Modern dancing and dancers

J. E. Crawford Flitch

Édition : BoD • Books on Demand GmbH, In de Tarpen 42,
22848 Norderstedt (Allemagne)
Impression : Libri Plureos GmbH, Friedensallee 273,
22763 Hamburg (Allemagne)
ISBN : 978-2-3225-5401-0
Dépôt légal : Septembre 2024

TABLE OF CONTENTS

INTRODUCTION

IT is not unlikely that when the art historian of the future comes to treat of the artistic activity of the first decade of the twentieth century, he will remark as one of its most notable accomplishments a renaissance of the art of the Dance.

That this renaissance is an accomplished fact, is a matter of common knowledge. Within a relatively short period there have appeared several great dancers, who must necessarily have been preparing themselves for a considerable time previously to their appearance, yet as it were in secret, without cognisance of one another, with a common aim, but without a common plan. Contemporaries in time, they have been as far removed in space as the East is from the West. In all movements which touch the spirit, this circumstance of the simultaneous but independent manifestation of a common impulse is at once the most general and the most unaccountable. The still small voice whispers into space and those of a delicate hearing hear and respond. We content ourselves by repeating the explanation, which is no explanation, that the movement is "in the air."

It follows, therefore, that he who sets out to relate adequately the story of the Dance in recent years should have qualified himself by being present at many different points, almost at one and the same time, ready to take account of its various exhibitions. Criticism of the Dance makes severer demands, at any rate physically, than criticism of literature. Dancers, even the most peripatetic, do not circulate with the same freedom as philosophers and novelists. Mahomet must always go to the mountain. It is true that all the roads of modern art lead to Paris, and some are continued as far as London. But the critic, even if he lies in wait at either of these centres, cannot always count on catching the bird of passage on the wing. To the quality of ubiquity I make no claim. And I may as well confess now as never that I saw Russia only when it came to Covent Garden. For the omission in this book, therefore, of a description of the performances of certain dancers, I have no better excuse to offer than the fact that I have never seen them. Silence in many cases must be taken to mean not my ignoring of their art, but my ignorance of it. I think I may claim, however, that the names that are omitted will be found to be famous rather on account of some personal quality in the dancer than on account of her influence on the development of the Dance.

There are other peculiar difficulties which beset the critic of the Dance. I do not refer to the difficulty of passing judgment upon a fugitive art that leaves nothing behind it but an echo of applause, for with the dancers of the past I have little concern. There is the difficulty of discriminating between the executant and the composer—a difficulty greater in dancing than in music, since the dancer is more than an executant of the art, she is herself the medium of it. In the popular eye she has in fact always quite eclipsed the choregrapher. Criticism is in doubt as to the measure of her share in the creation of the design—an uncertainty that cannot be resolved by any reference to a score. Further, it is in continual danger of being misled by the glamour of personal qualities —physical beauty, for example—which are strictly extraneous to the art. (Taglioni, it should be remembered, was probably the plainest as well as the greatest of dancers.) In no art, therefore, is personal prejudice established so readily or on grounds of such doubtful artistic validity.

The Dance enjoys no immunity from the clash of schools. Indeed, partisanship is the more bitter as principles of criticism are less determined. The respective upholders of the school of the ballet and of the natural or classical style of dancing are barely on speaking terms. To the advocates of the old school the new classical dancer is little better than a freak performer; to the austere classicist the ballet-dancer is but a smiling automaton, and both agree in refusing to recognise the skirt-dancer as a dancer at all.

To the exponents of conflicting styles I have endeavoured to do justice. If I have failed, it is of no great moment, since criticism of the Dance is still so inchoate that the opinion of the expert—and the responsibilities of his office I unhesitatingly refuse—has little more authority, except on questions of pure technique, than that of an expression of personal preference. I care little if the reader tears to tatters any hazardous conclusions upon which I have ventured. Such denials I expect. Almost I welcome them. But I care much if by anything that I have said the reader is provoked to formulate a serious criticism of his own and to refer his judgment to the abiding principles of art.

CHAPTER I

THE ANCIENT AND MODERN ATTI-
TUDE TOWARDS THE DANCE

I N latter, if not in former times, Dancing has commonly been regarded as the little sister of the Arts.

Gracious, wayward, beguiling, it has been indulged as the amusement of a trifling hour. It has ranked high among the amenities of life,
but low in the hierarchy of the sincere ministers of beauty. The liberal
arts have looked askance at its intrusion into their company. Dignity, seriousness of intention, fitness to express grave emotion, power to touch
the heights and depths of the spirit have been denied to it. It has suffered the disdain which is the habitual attitude of grown men towards
whatever appears to them to savour of the capricious and the childish.
Charm, of course, has been granted it—the butterfly charm of triviality.

It has been discussed earnestly only to be condemned. Little mercy
has the moralist ever shown to the art of the dance, but he has at least
done it this much justice—he has taken it seriously. To the puritan of all
times all the arts have been more or less suspect, but with regard to
dancing he has never had any doubts at all. He has damned it with bell,
book and candle. Indeed the logic of his own argument has left him no
alternative. For dancing is the life of the senses burning with its most
flamelike intensity. The appeal of all the arts is by their very nature sen-

suous, but in none is this appeal so direct and compelling as in the dance.

Happily the warping and misconceived morality of former generations is a thing of the past. The old opposition of sense to spirit is discredited as a false antithesis. It has been displaced by the more handsome creed that "all good things are ours, nor soul helps flesh more, now, than flesh helps soul." Beauty is a refiner's fire, and the beauty that enters in through the doorway of the senses cannot soil but only cleanse the spirit.

Nowadays the dance has less to fear from the hostility of the moralist than from the indifference of the artist. And perhaps the difficulty of restoring it to its ancient and rightful rank becomes thereby greater. It is easier to convince an angry opponent than the man who smiles indulgently at everything you have to say and then drops quietly off to sleep.

It is a true if unfortunate fact that the majority of people, at all events so far as the Anglo-Saxon race is concerned, not only do not appreciate the full beauty and meaning of dancing but show little or no desire ever to understand it. When they do not despise it as puerile, or actively resent it as immoral, they merely tolerate its performance as constituting the inevitable dull portion of a pantomime or the superfluous item in a music-hall programme. That dancing should ever have entered deeply into the religious and artistic life of nations is utterly inconceivable to them. To become proficient in the art for the sake of money or even for the love of admiration does not seem to them altogether unreasonable; but to dance as the world danced long ago, for the love of God —well, that falls into the portion of unintelligible ideas. Dancing has altogether ceased to play, indeed it never has played, a rôle of any importance in their lives. It means nothing more than paying occasionally to see the performance of some seven nights' wonder at a prominent music-hall, or, more usually, gyrating languidly on a beeswaxed floor to waltz time or bounding along kangaroo-like to the swinging melody of a popular two-step.

It is not the purpose of this book to present even an outline of the history of dancing, but in pleading for the "high seriousness" of the Dance as art it is desirable to consider for a moment the place which it once held in the ancient world—for this place, if I read the signs of the times aright, it is about to hold again.

The root of dancing is one with the root of all the arts, namely—ecstasy. Scorned as it has been by the sister arts of Music, Painting and Sculpture, it can boast a longer lineage than theirs, for the dance is more spontaneous than they. All the arts must needs be founded in emotion, but the moment of passion is usually long past before the labour of creation begins. The emotion is "recollected in tranquillity." But the raw material, if one may call it so, of the dance is the human body, and all human emotion expresses itself most spontaneously in bodily gesture. With children and simple peoples who have never learnt that it is incorrect to display their emotions, feeling is immediately translated into action. For a child words are never enough to express the heart's delight—as may be seen at any street corner when music is in the wind. The whole body becomes a lively instrument for joy to play upon. Joy for joy's sake only, however, is not yet art. "A child dancing for its own delight," says Ruskin, "a lamb leaping or a fawn at play, are happy and holy creatures; but they are not artists. An artist is a person who has submitted to a law which it was painful to obey, that he may bestow a delight which it is gracious to bestow." It is only when the emotion becomes self-conscious and seeks to communicate itself, that it evokes the help of formal rhythm—and where there is rhythm there is the alpha, if not the omega, of art.

This deep ecstasy out of which the dance springs, as a fountain from a well, is not necessarily joy. Often it is the ecstasy of love—for the dance, as Lucian said, is as old as love, the oldest of the gods. It may be the ecstasy of worship or the ecstasy of grief. From the nature of the emotion out of which it springs the dance takes its character—voluptuous, solemn, bacchic, mournful, as the case may be. Whenever the passions of primitive peoples were deeply moved, they evolved a dance to express them. In the mystic ritual dance they found some expression for that divine unrest, when the winds in the great forests or the serenity of the multitudinous stars strangely stirred the heart to a sense of the nearness of the spiritual order; when the triumphing warriors returned after driving back the onslaught of a hostile tribe, the sudden sense of relief from the fear of extermination could not but find vent in the dance of victory; around the bier of the chief, in sorrow, fear, and uncertainty, they dance the dances of death; in joy when they stored up for another year the kindly fruits of the earth they danced the harvest and vintage dances; and always and everywhere was danced the eternal pantomime of love.

In a passage which is none the less illuminating if its truth is perhaps imaginative rather than historical, Mr Max Beerbohm aptly illustrates the spontaneity of the dance and its development out of the ecstasy of some happy moment. "Some Thessalian vintner, say, suddenly danced for sheer joy that the earth was so bounteous; and his fellow-vintners, sharing his joy, danced with him; and ere the breath was spent they remembered who it was that had given them such cause for merry-making, and they caught leaves from the vine and twined them in their hair, and from the fig-tree and the fir-tree they snatched branches, and waved them this way and that, as they danced, in honour of him who was lord of these trees and of this wondrous vine. Thereafter this dance of joy became a custom, ever to be observed at certain periods of the year. It took on, beneath its joyousness, a formal solemnity, it was danced slowly around an altar of stone whereon wood and salt were burning—burning with little flames that were pale in the sunlight. Formal hymns were chanted around this altar. And some youth, clad in leopard's skin and wreathed with ivy, masqueraded as the god himself, and spoke words appropriate to that august character."

It was doubtless owing to its close connection with religion that the dance in ancient times was invested with so great dignity. It was a ceremonial before it became an amusement. Thus it is in its sacred character that we meet with the earliest instances of it. It had its place in the solemn rites of the Hebrew and the Egyptian. The Egyptian dances were full of esoteric meaning. The mystical circle of dancers round the altar interpreted the revolutions of the celestial bodies, the music of the spheres. It is significant that the name given to the dancing-women was *Awalim*, the wise or learned ones. Their dancing appears to have been no less elaborately technical than it was symbolic. From the painted records that have come down to us, it would appear that they were not unfamiliar with many of the movements of the modern ballet. There is little doubt that the Egyptian spectator of three or four thousand years ago delighted in the same pirouette as may be seen on the stage of St Petersburg and Milan to-day.

If Egypt was the seed-ground of the arts, it was in Greece that they flowered. As we should naturally expect, it was there that the art of rhythmic gesture achieved its most perfect expression. Thoroughly to appreciate the curious poses of the ancient dances of India and Egypt it would be necessary to understand the exact spiritual meaning of which those attitudes and gestures were but the symbol. But the dances of Greece, by their supreme beauty of movement and their power of rendering all the gamut of human emotion, are of universal appeal. There the dance escaped from its tutelage to religion and was made free of the kingdom of art. It had its part in that imperishable achievement of Greece—the revelation of the full glory and beauty of the "human form divine." In its turn it nourished the other arts. Greek sculpture drew no little of its inspiration from the dance, and its admirable gestures, thus caught in the fugitive moment and eternalised in stone, have enriched the world's heritage of beauty for all time.

In the Greek view, the dance was properly accompanied by music and song—song being the speech of music and dance the gesture of song. The three formed together a single imitative art, the aim of which was to present a definite emotion or idea. The story is told of Sostratus refusing to dance the dance of "Liberty" before the conqueror of his native town. "It would not be fitting for me," he said, "to dance the 'liberty' which my native town has lost." The Greeks never regarded dancing as a mere frivolous entertainment. From its power of affecting the emotions, and with them the character, they attributed to it a grave importance. In constructing his ideal republic, Plato went so far as to advocate its regulation by the State. The action of the State, let it be observed, was not to be a mere prohibition of degrading performances; it was actively to foster and prescribe the best dances with a view to elevating and perfecting the character of the citizens. Nothing could be stranger to a modern mind than this attitude of the ancient world to the dance; yet if it be true—and none I think will care to deny it—that dancing determines the emotions and that the emotions of a people determine its character, what could be more reasonable?

It is difficult to realise now to what an extent the whole life of the ancient world was coloured by the dance. It occupied as great a part as music, literature and the drama occupy in the life of to-day—perhaps a greater, for whereas in Western Europe there are many who care for none of these things, in Egypt, in Greece and in Rome, the dance touched the life of all classes and at every point. No ceremony of importance was conducted without dancing. It had its place in the rites of religion, at weddings and funerals, at private feasts and at public triumphs, in military exercises and in the theatre. It gave the theme to sculpture and painting. It went hand in hand with music. Indeed when we think of the ancient world we almost perforce think of it dancing. In the dance is summed up all the grace and gaiety of that old pagan life which was once lived on the sunlit shores of the Mediterranean, and which we are now wistfully and painfully beginning to attempt to recapture.

It is not a little strange that the dance should have fallen from its high estate as the handmaid of religion and hierarch of beauty to be the doubtful amusement of the café and the music-hall. In some measure undoubtedly its decline was due to the growing licentiousness in which it became involved. Homer dignified it with the epithet "irreproachable," but in Cicero's time it had already become so degenerate that he could say, "No sane man dances unless he is mad." Sallust was even more emphatic when he told a lady of his acquaintance that she danced with too much skill to be virtuous. The Catholic Church at first not only tolerated but actually incorporated the dance in Christian worship, and survivals of the ancient ritual dance exist in the churches of Spain to this day. But as the character of the dances became more equivocal they were condemned. Little by little the dance fell into disrepute.

But the moralist mistakes when he supposes that the dance stands in a different category from the other arts by reason of a special taint. Like all the other arts it reflects the morals of the time. Among peoples of simple faith and primitive virtue, the dance has always been marked by a certain strict and hieratic quality. It was so among the austere Romans of the early republic, and among the Christians of the first centuries. When manners decay, the dance becomes decadent also. It is not the dissoluteness of the dance that poisons the morals of the age; it is the corruption of the age that poisons the dance. The sensual character of so many eastern dances is the effect and not the cause of the sensuality of the race. If the dance suffers from any general relaxation of morality more swiftly and more disastrously than any of the other arts, it is because it expresses the emotions with such fidelity and emphasis. It is the most subtle and the most accurate index of the character of a people.

The dancing that is seen on the stage of to-day, however, is never reprehensible, and seldom even vulgar, and the fact that in former ages of looser living the dance became contaminated does not adequately explain the disesteem with which it appears, until recently, to have been regarded. The true reason seems to lie in the popular belief, not that dancing is less incorruptible, but that it is less serious than the other arts.

This fallacy—for such I take it to be—is doubtless due in part to the fact that when we speak of dancing we inevitably associate it with the ball-room. The word carries with it a train of images and recollections connected with the languorous cadence of waltz music, the perfume of conservatories, shady corners, champagne and ices, and the premature arrival of dawn. We can scarcely avoid thinking of it as merely the amusement of our lighter hours. But between the dancing of the ball-room and the dancing of art there is about as little connection as between the snow-man that children make on a winter's afternoon and the sculpture of the Parthenon. The one is an amusement, more or less graceful as the case may be, the other is an inspiration and a science. In the dancing of a mixed company at an evening party there is as little relation to art as there would be in an exhibition of pictures by a group of beginners, who had not yet mastered the elementary rules of drawing. If the performers derive any pleasure out of their respective exhibitions, there is an end of the whole matter and an excuse for it.

It is perhaps because everybody is more or less an amateur dancer that dancing has been lightly assumed to be a facile accomplishment which can easily be acquired after a few lessons, and a little practice. No misconception could be further from the truth. Probably there is no art that necessitates more prolonged and painful study. The dancer must be "caught young," if she is to excel. She must spend the whole of her youth in unremitting toil. She will be confronted with a bewilderingly elaborate technique. A steel resolution and a kind of passion for her calling must be hers, if she is not to flinch from the severity even of an elementary training.

Yet if dancing demanded nothing more than physical effort and mental application, it could not claim the seriousness of art. The dexterous execution of a number of intricate steps has no more value than that of any other *tour de force* . Soulless dancing has as little power to move the spectator as the feats of a clever acrobat. There can be no great dancing without emotion. Unless the dancer has the capacity for unusual emotion, and is also gifted with the power of emotional expression, which is the beginning and end of all great dancing, the performance never rises to anything more inspiring than a dreary and unpleasing display of mechanical accomplishment. If the dancer has nothing in her to express, she dances in vain. Great dancing demands deep sensibility and a subtle responsiveness to the strong rhythms of life, together with the power of translating these emotions into beauty of bodily movement. Dancing can be taught just as much and just as little as any other art. The great dancer is born.

But probably the seriousness of great art has been denied to dancing because of a common misapprehension as to what that seriousness consists in. It is almost always assumed that the seriousness of art depends upon its subject-matter. Serious art, it is supposed, must have a "message." It must be concerned with actual problems, social or religious. It must in some way be oppressed with the burden of contemporary life. But an art which has nothing to say, no conundrums to ask, no solutions to offer—what claim can that have upon our serious attention?

It is forgotten that it is not the subject that makes art serious or trivial, but the mood. There are problem pictures over which the public wrinkles its brows that are frivolous as a picture post-card from the point of view of art. And there are pictures of the bric-à-brac of a room, or a table spread for a meal, that are as grave as tragedy. It all depends upon the quality of the emotion that has gone to the making of them. The dance expresses the most serious thing in life—that is, ecstasy. All dull things are trivial. Art which has only the interest of contemporary problems is ephemeral, for when the problem is solved, the interest vanishes. The dance is the expression of the moods, and the moods are eternal. It has its source in passion, and where there is passion there is life at its utmost and seriousness at its highest.

In the present revival and development of the dance there is something at once significant and hopeful. It is not perhaps too conjectural to discern in it the hint of a reaction against one of the least agreeable tendencies in much of present-day art. It would seem that the arts are tending to become more and more enmeshed in contemporary affairs. They are exchanging the artistic conscience for a social conscience. When we ask for beauty they give us advice. Our serious novels are blue-books. Their writers appear to have no other interest than exposing the weak places of the social order. Drama has long since abandoned itself almost entirely to a painstaking study of marriage and divorce, and the problem picture we have always with us. Art has taken for its task the solution of the query, What's wrong with the world? It is furiously justifying its existence by hurrying to the rescue of the politician and the social reformer.

Into this vexed and anxious company of the arts the Dance strays a little timidly, bringing with it the serenity and grace of a less troubled age. It cannot produce the passport of discontent, without which it seems doubtful whether it is entitled to be admitted. It can contribute neither message nor criticism. It seeks not to reform us but only to please. It recalls us to the joy of life which the other arts had almost persuaded us to forget. It has but a single purpose—to quicken our pulses with beauty and to renew our life with its own untiring ecstasy.

CHAPTER II

THE RISE OF THE BALLET

A NY account of the modern renaissance of dancing must needs begin with the ballet. In one sense it is in the ballet that the dance attains its completest mode of expression. It may be regarded as the limit of its evolution, its most complex and elaborate statement. The more orderly sequence would be to trace the simpler forms of dancing through the various stages of their evolution until they arrive at their ultimate development in the ballet. The concern of this book, however, is not with the history of the dance, but rather with the interest which it has for the present time as an art-form. And it is with the dance as ballet that the awakening of this interest begins.

If the dance is essentially the art of democracy, springing out of the gladness of the crowd, the ballet in its origin is aristocratic. It was the diversion of courts before it became the delight of the populace.

In spite of its lavish production of masterpieces of art, the Renaissance would nevertheless have been incomplete without the ballet; for the ballet provided a perfectly fitting expression for two of the peculiar characteristics of the age—its love of pageant and its love of mythological allegory. If nothing akin to the ballet had ever existed in the world before, the fifteenth century would have been compelled to invent it. Invent it it did, and although there were precedents in the mysteries and interludes of the Middle Ages and in the old Roman saturnalia and pantomimi, the invention gave a new art-form to the world.

The ballet of the court was a mixed entertainment, consisting of poetry, music and dancing, in which princes and nobles took part. A poet was commissioned to write the verses, a musician to compose the score, a ballet-master to arrange the steps, and a painter to devise the artistic effects. These splendid court entertainments originated in Italy. The gorgeous spectacular display given in honour of the marriage of Galeazzo Visconti, Duke of Milan, in 1489, made a sensation not only in Italy but throughout Europe. The pageantry of the court ballet appealed to the heart of the splendour-loving Medici. Catherine de Medici introduced it into France.

It was in France that the *ballet de la cour* found its home. Henri IV. and Louis XIII. were both lovers of the ballet, while Louis XIV. may be said to have had a passion for it. The great cardinals, Richelieu and Mazarin, were its patrons. The first historian of the ballet, Le Père Ménestrier, gives an account of a "moral ballet" that was danced on Richelieu's birthday in 1634. The theme was *Truth, the Enemy of Seeming, upheld by Time* . It opened, we are told, with "a chorus of those False Rumours and Suspicions which usher in Seeming and Falsehood. They were represented by actors dressed as cocks and hens, who sang a dialogue, partly Italian, partly French, with a refrain of clucking and crowing. After this song the background opened and Seeming appeared, seated upon a huge cloud and accompanied by the Winds. She had the wings and the great tail of a peacock, and was covered with mirrors. She hatched eggs, from which issued Pernicious Lies, Deceptions, Frauds, Agreeable Lies, Flatteries, Intrigues, Ridiculous Lies, Jocosities, Little Fibs.

"The Deceptions were inconspicuously clad in dark colours, with serpents hidden among flowers. The Frauds, clothed in fowlers' nets, had bladders which they burst while dancing. The Flatteries were disguised as apes; the Intrigues as crayfishers, carrying lanterns on their heads and in their hands; the Ridiculous Lies as crippled beggars on wooden legs.

"Then Time, having put to flight Seeming with her train of Lies, had the nest opened from which these had issued; and there was disclosed a great hour-glass. And out of this hour-glass Time raised up Truth, who summoned the Hours and danced the grand ballet with them. "

But for the rather strident moral emphasis we seem to be breathing the atmosphere of Leicester Square! What has usually been regarded as a latter-day corruption of the ballet—the intrusion of a mass of irrelevant properties and stage-mechanism—appears to have been a kind of original sin which attached to it even in its origin.

In the reign of Louis XIV. the ballet passed definitely from the court to the theatre. In the earlier part of his reign the king himself frequently appeared in the ballet, usually taking the part of a god; but in course of time *le Grand Monarque* put on flesh and exchanged the rôle of an actor for that of a spectator. In 1661 was founded the *Académie royale de musique et de danse* , with Quinault as its first director, and the ballet henceforth took possession of the stage.

But before it assumed the form in which we know it, the ballet had to pass through several transformations. Originally the ballet, like the play, had been performed exclusively by men. The parts of bacchantes and nymphs had been taken by youths of slight and graceful build, and the use of masks, which at this time was general, assisted the convention. But in a ballet given at Saint-Germain in 1681, entitled *Le Triomphe de l'Amour* , Lulli, the composer, introduced the innovation of female dancers. The fashion became immediately popular. The part of the male dancer grew continually less important until in the ballets of the latter part of the nineteenth century it became altogether negligible, to be revived again in the Russian ballet of our own day.

The next step was the abolition of the mask. This did not take place until nearly a hundred years later. The custom of wearing the mask had its origin in the classical theatre and formed an essential part of the ballet from the Renaissance onwards. In 1772 Rameau's opera *Castor and Pollux* was given in Paris, the part of Apollo being taken by Gætano Vestris, who appeared, according to the fashion of the time, in a mask and an enormous full-bottomed black wig. One night he was unable to perform and Gardel, one of the leading dancers of the day, consented to act as a substitute, but only on condition that he was allowed to discard the mask and wig and appear in his own long fair hair. The happy innovation pleased the public and from that day the fashion of the mask was doomed.

But the character of the ballet was chiefly affected by the revolution in costume. In the earlier days of the ballet the dancers were dressed in the elaborate and fulsome costume of the period—the women in hooped petticoats falling to the ankle, with their powdered hair piled up a foot or more upon their heads, the men in long-skirted coats set out from their hips with padding. So long as this costume was worn the dance was necessarily confined almost entirely to the dignified and gliding movements of the minuet. It permitted none of the airy and intricate steps which are peculiar to the technique of the ballet proper. Noverre, the eighteenth-century *maître de ballet* , who is chiefly responsible for giving the ballet its present form, wrote as follows:—"I wish to reduce by three quarters the ridiculous paniers of our *danseuses* . They are opposed equally to the freedom, the quickness, and the prompt and animated action of the dance. They deprive the figure of its elegance and of the just proportions which it ought to possess. They diminish the beauty of the arms; they *bury* , so to speak, the graces. They embarrass and distract the dancer to such a degree that the movement of her panier sometimes occupies her more seriously than that of her limbs."

Mademoiselle de Camargo, the famous dancer of the first half of the eighteenth century, started the innovation in dress. She was the first to execute the entrechat, a light and brilliant step during the performance of which the dancer rapidly crosses the feet while in mid-air. In her dances, therefore, she took the precaution of wearing the *caleçon* , from which the tight-fitting fleshing of the ballet-dancer was subsequently evolved. This reform in costume brought about a transformation in the dance. When the limbs were freed from the thraldom of clothes, the movements of the ballet became swifter and more complex. Its technique was developed by the introduction of pirouettes, entrechats, jetés-battus, ballones. From an elegant accomplishment in which the lords and ladies of the court could take part, the ballet passed into a serious science, demanding the exclusive devotion of the performer. The reign of the amateur was over; that of the artist began.

To Noverre, whom Garrick called the "Shakespeare of dance," is chiefly due the creation of the ballet as an art-work, single, complete and harmonious in itself. Until his time it had existed principally as an auxiliary to opera. In the ballet-opera, which had reigned supreme on the stage hitherto, and has never in fact been entirely abandoned, the dances interpolated between the acts had borne little relation to the argument of the play. They were merely a diversion of quite secondary interest. The opera was not created for them but they for the opera. The revolution which Noverre effected was the creation of the *ballet d'action* , the unravelling of a plot by dancing and gesture pure and simple. For

Noverre the ballet was something much more serious than a mere saltatory display. It was an æsthetic composition which demanded the harmonious co-operation of a number of arts. "The master of the ballet," he said, "must study the works of painters and sculptors, he must know anatomy.... Everything which subserves the ends of painting must also be of service to the dance." He insisted upon the importance to the dancer of a knowledge of pantomime and himself studied closely the methods of Garrick. He deprecated the performance of the dance to any haphazard arrangement of lively airs. Music must be an integral portion of the ballet, written specially for it and informed with the spirit of the action. The costumes and the *décor* of the theatre must also be treated with a view to obtaining one single artistic effect. Thus Noverre succeeded in creating a new theatrical formula. He laid down the main lines along which the ballet has subsequently developed.

Although the English may claim to have been a nation of dancers in the old pre-Puritan days, dancing has certainly never been native to the English stage. The most brilliant of the dancers in the ballets that are produced upon the British stage to-day are foreign, and it has been so from the first. The ballet was late in coming to England. It sprang somewhat suddenly and dazzlingly to life upon the London stage in 1734. In that year Mademoiselle Sallé, who had already achieved fame in Paris, appeared at Covent Garden in the ballet of *Pygmalion and Galatea* . Like all the greatest dancers, she was a woman of distinguished personality. She counted Locke among her friends. Handel wrote specially for her the ballet of *Terpsichore* . Voltaire vacillated between his admiration of her and of her rival, Camargo, whom he apostrophised thus:

"Ah! Camargo, que vous êtes brillante!
Mais que Sallé, grand Dieu, est ravissante!
Que vos pas sont légers et que les siens sont doux!
Elle est inimitable et vous êtes nouvelle!
Les nymphes sautent comme vous,
Mais les Grâces dansent comme elle!"

Her dancing was full of expression and characterised by a certain simple dignity of motion; very rapid measures and eccentric movements she never attempted. She assisted in the reform of costume which Mademoiselle de Camargo had initiated. The *Mercure de France* noted that she appeared at Covent Garden "sans panier, sans jupe, sans corps, échevelée et sans aucun ornement sur la tête."

Her success was immediate and tumultuous. The public was frenzied with delight—whether at this first surprising revelation of the ballet or at the vision of the ravishing figure, "échevelée et sans jupe," it is impossible to say. And the enthusiasm of the British public in the eighteenth century appears to have had a Latin quality of abandon, which suggests the inference that the British character is not more but less emotional than it was. The crowds around the doors of the theatre, we are told, fought for a sight of the ballerina. The spectators had to force their way to the doors sword in hand. And, in the manner of Spaniards applauding a popular matador at a bull-fight, the Londoners showered upon the stage purses filled with guineas and jewels, which the cupids and satyrs of the troupe gathered up, keeping time to the music!

Seven years later England saw the greatest dancer of the century—perhaps the greatest *danseur* who has ever lived—Gætano Vestris. He was by birth an Italian and styled himself, with a better knowledge of his own accomplishments than of the pronunciation of the French language, "le diou de la danse." His amazing vanity was the source of innumerable anecdotes. "This century has produced but three great men," he used to say, "myself, Voltaire and Frederick the Great." One night in coming from the opera a portly lady happened to tread rather heavily upon his foot. She apologised, and hoped she had not hurt him very much. "Me, madam!" exclaimed the god of the dance, "me! You have only put Paris into mourning for a fortnight!" His son Auguste-Armand inherited almost all his father's talent. Gætano was wont to say of him, "If Auguste does not continue to float in mid-air, it is only out of consideration for his less gifted fellow-mortals."

As England never produced a great school of dancing, the vicissitudes of the ballet in this country fluctuated with its fortunes abroad. The French Revolution brought about the break-up, in 1789, of the *Communeauté des Maîtres à danser* founded by Louis XIV. Whenever the spirit of a people has been caught up in the great winds of emotion which sweep over the world with an invariable periodicity, the dance has always been the most immediate expression of the popular excitement. Perhaps France never danced so madly as during the Revolution. Paris danced between the massacres. The revolutionary spirit embodied itself in the Carmagnole. But it was the dance of the people, not the dance of art, that flourished during the Revolution. The *grand ballet* , in spite of an attempt to make it a vehicle for political ideas, languished. Among his multitudinous interests, however, Napoleon appears to have included a concern for the art of dancing, and in his enumeration of the requisites of his Egyptian expedition "a troupe of ballet girls" figures among the quota of cannon and ammunition.

A consequence of the Revolutionary and Napoleonic wars, which does not usually figure in the pages of the historian, was that the supply of Parisian *danseuses* for the English stage was cut off for a generation or more. Even for some years after the peace, the French were inclined to keep their best performers for them selves and sent over to England only their discarded favourites. The golden period of the ballet in England began in the twenties of the nineteenth century and lasted until the fifties. In 1821 a determined effort was made to secure some of the most dazzling stars of the Parisian ballet. The difficulties to be overcome were not light, for, as the Parisian dancers were trained in an academy maintained by the state, none could leave the country without the permission of the Government. The British ambassador was himself charged with the negotiations. After many pourparlers, a treaty was drawn up, signed and sealed, by which one of the two high-contracting parties agreed to loan to the other two first and two second dancers from the Academy, while the other in return was to pledge itself not to attempt to import any other dancer without the Academy's consent.

The first two to arrive were the *danseur* Albert and the *première danseuse* Noblet, who were engaged at a salary of £1700 and £1500 respectively. They took London by storm. They were the idols of society; the fashionable world could think and talk of nothing but their dancing. The reign of the ballet had begun. Already in the first season the cost of the ballet exceeded that of the opera by some £2000. No other form of theatrical art approached the ballet in popularity. The King's Theatre, afterwards transformed and renamed Her Majesty's, kept a permanent *corps de ballet* . The Haymarket, Her Majesty's, and Covent Garden nightly drew crowded houses to witness displays of the most accomplished dancing that had ever been seen on the English stage. With the advent of Taglioni enthusiasm reached its utmost limits.

For about a quarter of a century England was enraptured with the ballet. It is impossible for us to attempt to envisage the early Victorian era without the ballet entering prominently into the picture. It appears to present the just embodiment of the formal but naïve gaiety, the untroubled imagination, the somewhat vulgarian æstheticism of the age. The ballerina, with her straightly parted hair, her rose wreath, her innocent affectations, is the complement to the whiskered dandy of the D'Orsay period. The ballet seems to be as closely attached to early Victorianism as are Louis Quinze furniture or Chelsea porcelain shepherdesses to their respective periods. It is not altogether easy for us to regard it otherwise than as a revival. Even now the ballet, in its costumes, its music, its *décor*, is not free from a tendency to hark back to the thirties and forties of the last century.

CHAPTER III

THE HEYDAY OF THE BALLET

"W ILL the young folks ever see anything so charming, anything so classic, anything like Taglioni?" The question occurs in "Pendennis," and how shall we answer it?

The dance is the most fugitive of the arts. Time makes but slow headway in obliterating a picture or a statue, and a verse is too elusive for his grasp; but the dancer's art dies with her, or rather the dancer herself outlives it. Painting may preserve some phantom of her grace, but the soul of the grace is in the motion which it cannot represent. The dancer lives only in hearsay, in the memory of spectators, and when the last eye-witness is gone she is no more than a name to posterity. Taglioni's is perhaps the greatest name in the annals of dancing, but a comparison of her art with that of her successors of the present day is well-nigh impossible. We can only judge of her genius by the echoes of the applause which have not even yet quite died away.

Marie Taglioni was born in Stockholm in 1804. Her father was an Italian, her mother a Swede. Her name was already well known in the world of the theatre, as her father was a *maître de ballet* and two of her aunts had been celebrated dancers. But although she was born into the tradition, she appears not to have been formed by nature to be a dancer. When her father took her as a child to see Coulon, a famous dancing-master at the beginning of the last century, the master turned to him and said, "What the devil am I to make of that little hunchback!" But by years of assiduous training she overcame any defect of form that may have been hers by birth.

She made her début in 1822 at Vienna in a ballet which her father had composed specially for her, entitled *Réception d'une jeune Nymphe à la Cour de Terpsichore* . Her success there was immediate and it was not long before the young dancer became one of the "stars" of the Opera. When she appeared in Paris, however, five years later, in *Le Sicilien* , her reception was somewhat cold. Perseverance was one of Taglioni's characteristics and she determined to achieve the conquest of the French capital, a measure which was even more necessary then than now to the dancer who aspired to universal fame. She succeeded and her success there set the seal upon her artistic fortunes. She appeared successively in *La Vestale* , *Mars et Vénus* , *Fernand Cortez* , *Les Bayadères* , and *Le Carnaval de Venise* . She was acclaimed as the greatest dancer of the day. In *La Sylphide* she achieved a triumph which resounded throughout the whole of Europe.

From Paris she extended her conquests to London, where she first appeared in 1830 in Didelot's ballet, *Flore et Zéphire* . An incident which happened during her stay in London is significant of the discipline upon which her father insisted. He had a small sloping stage erected in his daughter's room, in order that she might practise her steps every night. A gentleman occupying the floor below sent word that the dancer was on no account to interrupt her practice from fear of disturbing him. Philippi Taglioni resented the courtesy. "Tell the gentleman," he said, "that I, her father, have never yet heard my daughter's step—if ever that should happen, I would have no more to do with her!"

She had been brought to England as a counter-attraction to the famous Lablache and Malibran, then in the zenith of their popularity in Italian opera. She at once became the idol of the British public. The theatre was literally besieged on those nights when she was announced to appear. It was in England that she found a public ever ready to cry her praises when her fame was being seriously challenged by younger rivals abroad.

She received a salary paid to no other dancer in the world. She demanded and obtained a hundred pounds a night, in addition to which several of her relations had to be financed as well. An inordinate love of money was one of the least favourable of her traits. One night the manager of Her Majesty's Theatre was compelled to come before the curtain to apologise for the fact that the ballet had not begun, because Taglioni, sitting in her dressing-room, refused to appear on the stage until a large sum of money had been paid her on account. Her temper behind the scenes intimidated even the most hardened manager. One evening, when the male dancer Perrot happened to receive a greater amount of applause than herself, she refused to continue the performance, and accused everybody right and left of having plotted to dethrone her. But she had only to dance and everything was forgiven her. She was the spoilt child of the play-going world.

Apart from the glamour which she cast over her contemporaries, Taglioni exercised a considerable influence over the development of the ballet. She finally freed it from the remains of the eighteenth-century artificiality and affectation which had given a certain grotesqueness to most of the dancers before her time. She helped to do away with the rather heavy pseudo-classicism of the earlier ballet; her dancing was Catholic, if the expression may be allowed, rather than pagan. She adopted a quality of restraint in her dress and manner. She danced in a long tunic of white silk-muslin, which reached almost to her ankles and fell in graceful folds from her figure. Indeed so long was her skirt that when she was dancing in St Petersburg it is said that the Czar was compelled to leave his box and take a seat in the stalls. Her hair was dressed in the style of the

Madonna, falling back severely on either side and encircled by a wreath of roses. Her eyes were usually downcast, her attitude demure.

As a woman she had few if any pretensions to real beauty; her jaw was too square, her features too pronounced. Her form also came short of physical perfection. But apart from her genius for dancing she possessed an extraordinary charm of manner. With her modest appearance, her unadorned simplicity, her virginal air of innocence, she seemed to bring a new atmosphere into the ballet. She was remarkable in winning the whole-hearted admiration of her own sex. One of her male acquaintances once asked her if she would not modify her costume so as to display more of the grace of her figure. Her reply is characteristic. "Sir," she asked, "are you married?" He replied that he was. "Well," retorted the dancer, "I dance not for you, but for your wife and daughters."

Her dancing was marked by an entire absence of the false consequence and bombast of carriage and manner which appear to have characterised most of the dancers of the time. Its chief note was a certain spirituality. Taglioni appealed to the spirit rather than to the sense. She seemed less a being of flesh and blood than some creature of the spiritual order, always about to take wing and soar away from the earth. Her dance was remarkable in suggesting flight. One of her most wonderful attitudes was an *arabesque* which gave her the appearance of actually flying. She completely lacked the fire and abandon of her great rival Fanny Elssler. Her dance was chastened and aspiring rather than voluptuous and intoxicating. "*La Sylphide* marks a ballet epoch," says Mr Chorley, the author of "Musical Recollections," "as a work that introduced an element of delicate fantasy and fairyism into the most artificial of all dramatic exhibitions, one which to some extent poetised it. After *La Sylphide* were to come *La Fille de Danube* and *Giselle* (containing some of Adolphe Adam's best music), *L'Ombre* and a score of ballets, in which the changes were rung on naiad and nereid life, on the ill-assorted love of some creatures of the elements for an earthly mortal. The purity and ethereal grace of Mademoiselle Taglioni's style suggested the opening of this vein, as it also founded a school of imitators. Her mimic powers, however elegant, were limited. Her face had few changes. Her character dances, as in *Guillaume Tell* and *La Bayadère* , were new and graceful; but their seduction and piquancy were to be outdone. When she touched our English ground, however, the sylph excited as much enthusiasm as the most idolised songstress can now evoke."

Perhaps not a little of her popularity was due to the fact that the age saw in her the concrete expression of the qualities which it most esteemed. The emotions she expressed were placid, not of the

MARIE TAGLIONE

AS *La Sylphide*

soul-shattering order. She was the gracious incarnation of the early Victorian ideal.

Unfortunately, however, the virtue of domesticity was sadly lacking in her private life. The blame however rests entirely with her husband. In 1832 she married Count Gilbert des Voisins, but the union was of brief duration, for almost on the morrow of the wedding she was forgotten by him. She met him twenty years later, so it is related, at a dinner given by the Duc de Morny. When he appeared she demanded of Morny to know why he had invited her to dine in such disreputable company. After dinner Gilbert de Voisins, who feared nothing, not even his wife, had the audacity to ask to be introduced to Marie Taglioni. "I fancy, monsieur," she remarked, "that I had the honour of being presented to you in 1832!"

Taglioni lived long enough to taste all the bitterness of the discarded favourite. When she became too old to practise her art, and other less gifted but more youthful dancers usurped her place, she passed swiftly into oblivion. At the last, the dancer who had been wont to receive the homage of kings and princes, and the adulation of the public of two continents, remained without a friend. She lost all her fortune and in her distress was compelled to give lessons in dancing and deportment. "It was a sad sight," says Henri Bauer, "to see her, a white-haired old lady, escorting a bevy of English schoolgirls in Hyde Park in the winter, at Brighton in the summer, or, accompanied by a little old Italian, teaching dances and court curtseys to the proud daughters of the gentry."

"I would be young again to dance," she said to a friend who had asked her if she would like to live her life all over again, "I would be young again to dance—but not from any love of life, not to repeat any other experiences and pleasures."

Marie Taglioni died at Marseilles in 1884.

The passion for the ballet in the nineteenth century reached its climax in the amazing rivalry between Taglioni and Fanny Elssler. The appearance of the Austrian dancer brought about a schism in the cult of Taglioni. It was fought out with all the fury of the *odium theologicum* . The two claimants to the sceptre of the dance divided the world into rival camps. And how shall posterity, to whom both are little more than shadowy names, make a just award?

Fanny Elssler was born in Vienna in 1810. Her father was Haydn's copyist and factotum, and the composer interested himself greatly in the beginnings of her career. It began early, for at the age of six she was dancing at a little Viennese theatre in one of the *ballets d'enfants* then in vogue. She was first taught in the old, stereotyped style of ballet-dancing which was revolutionised by Taglioni and fell into disfavour about 1830. Her studies were completed in Italy, where she passed a great part of her life. She first came into note at Naples and danced her way through Italy to Berlin and London. Paris she reserved for her latest conquest. It was when she was dancing at Her Majesty's Theatre that Véron, the director of the Paris opera, saw Elssler and immediately secured her for the next operatic season. The English at this time, in spite of their enthusiasm for ballet, appear to have lacked the artistic perception to discover a dancer for themselves. A great reputation abroad was the only royal road to success on the London stage. And so it was that they failed to discover what a genius they had in their midst until it was too late and the new dancer was being acclaimed in Paris as a serious rival to the incomparable Taglioni.

Fanny Elssler had the advantage over Taglioni in possessing a beauty so striking that she had only to appear upon the stage when a kind of passionate shudder swept through the audience, more significant than the loudest tumult of applause. Her beauty was of the sort that consists less in the parts than in the harmony of the whole. No single feature imperiously demanded the homage of the eye, but her perfect unity was like that of a Greek statue. Her hands and feet were perfectly adjusted to her limbs; her head was attached to her body by the purest lines of neck and shoulder; her arms were supple and alert; her strength never trespassed upon her grace. Her form had a suggestion of masculine beauty. She has been compared to that ravishing chimera of Greek art, the son of Hermes and Aphrodite, whose body was united with the nymph of a river while bathing. This ambiguous quality in her beauty expressed itself in all her actions. Even in the yielding form and seductive charm of the dancer there was a hint of the agility, the brusque alertness, the steel muscles of the young athlete.

She added to her grace of movement an exceptional command of expression. Her eyes were lit with a certain malicious voluptuousness; when she smiled a trace of irony played about her lips. In repose her face was like a marble mask; in action it was capable of expressing the whole range of the emotions, from tragic grief to the maddest gaiety.

The début of Fanny Elssler in Paris proved to be the great sensation of the season. Curiosity had already been aroused by the rumour of her liaison with the Duc de Reichstadt, the son of the first Napoleon—a rumour wholly baseless as she had never even seen the youth. Nevertheless the imagination of the large body of Bonapartists then living in Paris was so fired that they made her début the occasion of a great demonstration against Louis-Philippe.

The ballet in which she appeared was founded upon Shakespeare's *Tempest*. "Tout-Paris" flocked to the theatre. But of all the notabilities the figure that excited most interest was that of a woman sitting alone in a small box on the right of the stage. It was Marie Taglioni. She knew, and everybody else knew, that Véron, the manager, had brought the newcomer over from London specially to dethrone her. With a somewhat scornful disdain she had come to take stock of her rival. Perhaps she anticipated her discomfiture; in any case she can scarcely have been prepared for the suddenness of her triumph. The new dancer did not appear until the second of the two acts. Her success was never in doubt for an instant. Her very first dance created a profound impression, and the enthusiasm at the close of the performance knew no limits. As she came before the curtain to acknowledge the thunder of applause, many eyes were turned towards Taglioni's box. It is said that the tears were streaming down the face of the Italian dancer.

The newspapers of the following morning without exception published eulogies of the débutante. The general public, however, was almost evenly divided between the merits of the rival schools. Open war was now declared between the two dancers. Taglioni's reply was to revive the ballet of *La Sylphide*, in which she had achieved her greatest triumph and captured the heart of the Parisian public years before. The result was that the pendulum of popularity swung back violently in her favour. The admirers of the Austrian retorted by throwing ridicule upon the affected innocence of Taglioni's style, which after Elssler's dancing appeared altogether lacking in passion and fire.

The war between the Taglionists and the Elsslerites continued for years. Nothing like it had been known since the rivalry of Pylades and Bathyllus, when every Roman was either a Bathyllian or a Pyladian, or the contests between the reds and the blues of the circus in Byzantium. The Taglionists claimed the victory and the Elsslerites considered their opponents vanquished. Each party strove to vindicate the perfection of one or other of two utterly opposed styles of dancing. They were, in fact, incomparable with one another. Taglioni's dancing was spiritual, while that of Elssler was distinctly of the terrestrial order. Elssler was warmly human, passionate, dramatic; Taglioni when dancing seemed scarcely to belong to the earth. Elssler introduced into the ballet an abandon, fire, petulance, temperament, which the strict limits of art seemed all too narrow to contain. The classical pirouette provided no adequate outlet for her passion; she demanded the freer motions of the South and East. She brought to the dance the ardour of the meridian, the *fougue espagnole* . She was at her best in Spanish dances, especially in the famous *cachucha* , which she made entirely her own. Théophile Gautier said that he had seen Rosita Diez, Lola, the best dancers of Madrid, of Seville, of Cadiz, of Granada, and the gipsies of Albaycin, but he had never seen anything to approach the *cachucha* as danced by Fanny Elssler.

Chorley, the English critic, also agrees in attributing a unique character to her dancing. "The exquisite management of her bust and arms (one of the hardest things to acquire in dancing) set her apart from everyone whom I have ever seen before or since. Nothing in execution was too daring for her, nothing too pointed . If Mademoiselle Taglioni flew, she flashed. The one floated on to the stage like a nymph, the other showered every sparkling fascination round her like a sorceress. There was more, however, of the Circe than of the Diana in her smile."

If Taglioni embodied the ideals of early Victorian England, Elssler was the incarnation of the Romantic movement of the Continent. She was the new wine that was too strong for the old wineskins of classical tradition. She had in her blood the northern enthusiasm for the South which was the keynote of the movement. She drew her inspiration from Spain, and so her spirit was attuned to that of the Romantics, whose gaze also was towards the Pyrenees. She falls naturally into line with a school which cared more for tumultuous movement than for classical repose, for colour more than for form, for intense immediate sensation more than for considered and reflective statement.

Some of the magic of Elssler's dancing is caught in Gautier's description of her appearance in the Spanish ballet *El Diablo Cojuelo* . "Clad in a skirt of rose-coloured satin clinging closely to the hips, adorned with deep flounces of black lace, she comes forward with a bold carriage of her slender figure, and a flashing of diamonds on her breast. Her leg, like polished marble, gleams through the frail net of the stocking. Her small foot is at rest, only awaiting the signal of the music to start into motion. How charming she is with the large comb in her hair, the rose behind her ear, her flame-like glance and her sparkling smile! At the extremity of her rose-tipped fingers tremble the ebony castanets. Now she darts forward; the castanets commence their sonorous clatter; with her hands she seems to shake down clusters of rhythm. How she twists! how she bends! what fire! what voluptuousness of motion! what eager zest! Her arms seem to swoon, her head droops, her body curves backwards until her white shoulders almost graze the ground. What charm of gesture! And with that hand which sweeps over the dazzle of the footlights would not one say that she gathered all the desires and all the enthusiasms of those who watch her?"

The climax of the famous Taglioni-Elssler rivalry came when, in defiance of all precedent, Elssler appropriated the most celebrated of her predecessor's ballets. Taglioni had made her name famous throughout the world in *La Sylphide* . She had made the part so exclusively her own that the pretension of any other dancer to appear in it seemed little less a desecration than an impertinence. The announcement that Elssler had determined to challenge her rival on her own ground fell like a bombshell in the ranks of Taglionists and Elsslerites alike. But in this instance the ambition of the Austrian dancer overshot the mark. The part demanded the ethereal grace which none but Taglioni possessed. Elssler's performance was almost a failure. Deeply chagrined at the reverse, she left soon afterwards for America.

Théophile Gautier lamented in a whimsical strain her loss to Europe. "Ungrateful, she has left us," he wrote, "she has gone away to America, to the savages and the Yankees, whom she has wrought to such a madness with the clatter of her castanets and the swaying of her hips that senators drag her carriage through the streets and whole populations follow her with cheers and fanfares."

In America Elssler aroused a delirium of enthusiasm which put her brightest European triumphs into the shadow—for America appears to have a capacity for worship which the older continent has exhausted and for two glorious years Elssler was its goddess. She was received by the President of the Union himself, Van Buren, surrounded by his ministers. During her visit to Washington the wheels of legislation and public business ceased for a time to revolve. It was decided that Congress should only meet on those days when Fanny was not dancing. Dollars rained upon her. Daily she received bizarre and costly presents—massive gold cigar-boxes and chemises embroidered with precious stones. "At present she possesses fragments of the coffins of Napoleon and George Washington," her companion, Catherine Prinster, gravely related—suggesting a future pregnant with grim possibilities. When she returned from the theatre at night crowds followed her with blaring bands; flowers and carpets were spread for her carriage to pass over; illuminated arches were raised to brighten her progress. The very handkerchiefs which she had used after dancing were fought for as precious relics; the water in which she had dipped her hands was preserved in bottles; and her admirers drank her health in champagne out of the shoes in which she had danced the delirious *cachucha* .

On her return from America Elssler paid many visits to Italy, appearing for several successive seasons at La Scala, in Milan. There she was caught up in the vortex of international politics. The school of ballet which had been founded at La Scala in 1811 was encouraged by the Austrian Government, partly in the hope of providing a safety-valve for that effervescence of enthusiasm without which an Italian populace appears unable to exist. The glories of the ballet, it was supposed, would prevent the popular mind from dwelling too insistently upon the glories of Italian independence. Everywhere throughout the city was seen the portrait of the ballerina. The theatre was decorated with roses when she appeared. Listening to the cheers with which she was received, Radetzky, the governor, rubbed his hands gleefully and said, "At any rate they are not plotting any revolutions now!"

1848, however, was the year of Elssler's Sedan. Revolution was in the air and the governor sent for Elssler to dance it away. The ballet which was selected was Perrot's *Faust* . In the first scene, all the members of the *corps de ballet* appeared wearing a medal representing Pius IX., the new liberal Pope, giving his benediction to a united Italy. Unfortunately Elssler regarded the demonstration as directed specially against herself as an Austrian. Behind the scenes she told the director that she refused to go on the stage again unless the offending medals were taken off. The order was given accordingly. The audience was speedily informed of the cause of the change, and when the *première danseuse* next appeared on the stage she was received with a tempest of hisses. Though she never danced with greater brilliance and grace, the only response to her endeavours to conciliate the anger of the spectators was a sepulchral silence from the stalls and a running fire of insults from the gallery. Bravely she smiled upon them, but the patriots forgot the dancer in the Austrian and replied with cries of *Basta! Basta!* She fainted. At last the idol had fallen. She was looked upon merely as the instrument of the foreign domination. She tore up her contract with the impresario and returned to Vienna.

Elssler retired in 1851. The end of her career was in striking contrast to that of Taglioni. In spite of a prodigal charity she had accumulated a fortune of a quarter of a million. She preserved the freshness of her youth to the last. In society she was always the most elegant figure. She was beloved by the poor. In Milan it had been her wont to send all the flowers she received to be placed before a statue of the Virgin in the Church of San Fedele. In Vienna she was as famous for her charities as for her dancing. The final curtain was rung down upon the long rivalry of the two dancers in 1884, when the Austrian capital went into mourning for the death of Elssler and Taglioni died poor and forgotten in Marseilles.

Théophile Gautier, perhaps the most discriminating critic of the ballet, said of Fanny Elssler that she was the most vital, the most precise, the most intelligent dancer who ever graced the boards of the stage. Her dancing had not the exquisite lightness, the purity of gesture and attitude, the ethereal qualities of Taglioni; but in dramatic significance, in fire, passion and imagination, her art never has been, and probably never will be, equalled.

After the disappearance of the two immortal rivals, who was to carry on the great tradition? Gautier gives us the answer: "For a long time," he writes, "women had said—What can come after the misty grace, the decent abandon of Taglioni? For a long time men had asked—What can come after the provocative verve, the spirited and wanton caprice, the purely Spanish fire of Fanny Elssler? Carlotta Grisi has come—light and chaste as the first, vivacious, joyous and precise as the second, only with the inestimable advantage of counting no more than twenty-two Aprils and of being fresh as a nosegay wet with dew."

Carlotta Grisi was born in 1821 in a remote mountain village of Istria. At the age of seven she was dancing in Milan at La Scala, where Perrot discovered her. She profited by the excellent tuition of the great *maître de ballet* , and subsequently danced in Naples, Venice, Vienna and London. Those who witnessed her

CARLOTTA GRISI

IN *La Péri*

début at the Paris Opera House in *Zingaro* wondered whether she would become more famous as a dancer or a singer. Her voice was so pure and just that Malibran, the famous operatic singer, advised her to devote herself entirely to music. But guided by that inner voice which speaks infallibly to all great artists she decided to remain faithful to the dance. She was the *première danseuse* at the Paris Opera from 1841 to 1848.

Grisi was of medium height; her feet exquisitely shaped; her limbs clean, nervous, of great purity of line; her complexion so fresh that the only use she made of rouge was to revive the fading colour of her pink dancing-shoes. Her expression had a childish *naïveté* , a gay and communicative happiness. This fresh and almost infantile gaiety was the keynote of her dancing. When she appeared upon the stage she seemed to bring with her the freshness of her native mountain air and the sparkle of the sun upon the snow.

What *La Sylphide* was to Taglioni and *El Diablo Cojuelo* to Elssler, the ballet of *Giselle* was to Grisi. It was the work of three famous men: Heine furnished the subject, Gautier wrote the scenario and Adolphe Adam composed the music. The scene was laid among the mountains, at the season of the gathering of the grapes. At the vintage fête Giselle danced with such unwearied zest that her mother said to her: "Luckless child, you will dance yourself to death, and when you die you will become a will-o'-the-wisp. You will go to the ball at midnight in a robe of moonshine and with bracelets of dew-pearls on your cold white feet. You will entice lost travellers into the fatal circle and you will lead them, all warm and breathing, into the icy waters of the lake. You will be a vampire of the dance!" Grisi's most marvellous dance was her dance of death and resurrection as a fairy-spirit. Giselle sickened with despair of love until she lost her reason. Her madness did not take the form of an Ophelia-like melancholy. She began to dance, she danced ever more swiftly and furiously. As she danced, a gleam of reason came to her; she remembered her sorrow and, resolving to end it and her life together, she ran upon the point of a sword. Wounded to death she went on dancing swooningly, and after some last disordered steps died in a marvellous kind of choregraphic agony. In the next act came her no less wonderful dance of resurrection. After she is dead, her grave in the forest is discovered by the fairy troop. She is awaked by magic from her long sleep. She rises and dances with a tottering motion like one still dazed with dream. Gradually her limbs forget the contraction of the grave-clothes; the cool air of the night and the light of the moon restore her gaiety; delightedly she takes possession of space and abandons herself to the ecstasy of her new fairy life. Grisi made of the ballet a true poem, a kind of choregraphic elegy, full of tender charm. More than one spectator who had never expected to be moved by a *rond-de-jambe* or *arabesque* was surprised by tears. Henceforth the part was impossible for any other dancer and the name of Carlotta became inseparable from that of *Giselle* .

The perfect art of these three dancers, Taglioni, Elssler and Carlotta Grisi, raised the ballet during the term of their fame to the highest degree of excellence which it had ever reached. To their names must be added those of Fanny Cerito, who was known in Italy as the "fourth Grace," and Lucille Grahn, who according to some critics combined the ideal form of Taglioni with the realism of Elssler and the sprightliness of Carlotta Grisi. These two dancers would probably have been without a rival in any less brilliant epoch than that of the marvellous forties.

In England the ballet may be said to have reached its apogee on the 12th of July 1845. On that memorable day four of the foremost dancers of the age, Marie Taglioni, Carlotta Grisi, Fanny Cerito and Lucille Grahn, danced a *pas de quatre* before Queen Victoria. The bringing together of such a glittering constellation of stars on a single stage is best told in the words of the impresario who conceived and accomplished the achievement.

"With such materials in my grasp as the four celebrated *danseuses* , Taglioni, Carlotta Grisi, Cerito and Lucille Grahn, it was my ambition to unite them all in one striking *divertissement* . But ambition, even seconded by managerial will, scarcely sufficed to put such a project into execution. The government of a great state was but a trifle

FANNY CERITO

IN *Ondine*

compared to the government of such subjects as those whom I was
supposed to be able to command; for these were subjects who considered

49

themselves far above mortal control, or, more properly speaking, each was a queen in her own right—alone, absolute, supreme.... But there existed difficulties even beyond a manager's calculations. Material obstacles were easily overcome. When it was feared that Carlotta Grisi would not be able to leave Paris in time to rehearse and appear for the occasion, a vessel was chartered from the Steam Navigation Company to waft the sylph at a moment's notice across the Channel; a special train was engaged and ready at Dover; relays of horses were in waiting to aid the flight of the *danseuse* all the way from Paris to Calais. In the execution of the project the difficulty was again manifold. Every twinkle of each foot in every *pas* had to be nicely weighed in the balance, so as to give no preponderance. Each *danseuse* was to shine in her peculiar style and grace to the last stretch of perfection; but no one was to outshine the others, unless in her own individual belief. Lastly, the famous *Pas de Quatre* was composed with all the art of which the distinguished ballet-master, Perrot, was capable.

"All was at length adjusted. Satisfaction was in every mind; the *Pas de Quatre* was rehearsed—was announced; the very morning of the event had arrived; no further hindrances were expected. Suddenly, while I was engaged with the lawyers in my room, poor Perrot rushed unannounced into my presence in a state of intense despair. He uttered frantic exclamations, tore his hair, and at last found breath to say that all was over—the *Pas de Quatre* had fallen to the ground, and could never be given. With difficulty the unfortunate ballet-master was calmed down to a sufficient state of reason to be able to explain the cause of his anguish. When all was ready, I had desired Perrot to regulate the order in which the separate *pas* of each *danseuse* should come. The place of honour, the *last* in such cases, as in regal processions, had been ceded without over-much hesitation to Mademoiselle Taglioni. Of the remaining ladies who claimed equal rights, founded on talent and popularity, neither would appear before the others. 'Mon Dieu!' exclaimed the ballet-master, 'Cerito will not begin before Carlotta, nor Carlotta before Cerito; there is no way to make them stir—all is finished.' 'The solution is easy,' said I; 'let the *oldest* take her unquestionable right to the envied position.' The ballet-master smote his forehead, smiled assent, and bounded from the room upon the stage. The judgment of the manager was announced. The ladies tittered, laughed, drew back, and were now as much disinclined to accept the right of position as they had been before eager to claim it. The order of the ladies being settled, the *Grand Pas de Quatre* was finally performed on the same night before a delighted audience, who little knew how nearly they had been deprived of their promised treat."

It is scarcely possible now to conceive the excitement which this performance created. It overshadowed for the time every other national interest. The reports were eagerly awaited by the Continent. Foreign courts received accounts of it enclosed in the official despatches. It was a European event.

But even in the heyday of its prosperity there was a premonition of the waning of the popularity of ballet. In the very year of this triumphant dance, Jenny Lind was heard for the first time in London. The human voice was about to drive the speechless ballet from the theatre.

CHAPTER IV

THE DECLINE OF THE BALLET

T HE history of every art-form is a record of growth, maturity, decay and rebirth. The life of art appears to be subject to cycles, the recurrence of which is as certain and as inexplicable as those of nature. When perfect facility of execution has been attained, the period of decline is at hand. Nothing is left to the artist but to attempt to elaborate forms that are already perfect. The mode of art which has reached its zenith has expressed everything which the age had to say through that particular medium. Executive skill may still remain but the creative spirit is no longer present to inform it. The result almost necessarily is a barren accomplishment which has ceased to have any significance. The artist seeks to conceal his lack of inspiration by purely mechanical dexterity. He produces that over-elaboration of detail which is the sure mark of decadent art. An art which is fullblown can never begin to bud again until it has drawn up the sap of a new emotion and again has something significant to express to the age.

The history of the ballet has shown no exception to this general law. After its brilliant efflorescence in the second quarter of the last century it passed into a season of decay. The first cause naturally was the disappearance of the dancers of genius whose careers have been briefly sketched in the last chapter. When she danced in the famous *Pas de Quatre* in 1845 Marie Taglioni had already passed her fortieth year; Fanny Elssler never danced after 1851; Carlotta Grisi and Cerito quitted the stage shortly afterwards. More than any other art, dancing lives by the genius of its exponents. Unlike painting, sculpture and literature, it leaves no permanent record behind it—only a name and a reputation. If there is a gap in the sequence of great dancers, there ceases to be any living art to serve as a source of inspiration for the next generation. The traditional methods may be carried on, but without the living exponent they rapidly become lifeless.

The great dancers had no successors of equal genius. The French and Italian schools, which in a single generation had produced so many of the world's most famous dancers, suddenly became sterile. All the great dancers of the nineteenth century were grounded upon the Italian method. In Milan they mastered the technique; in Paris, where the ballet was closely connected with the best artistic life of the day, they seem to have found the inspiration of art. Now, the teaching genius of both schools appeared to have deserted them. Dancers still flooded the theatres of Europe; most of them had been through the finishing school of the French capital; they modelled their style upon the great Taglioni and Elssler traditions; but their achievement was stale and unbeautiful. The attitudes with which Taglioni had enraptured the whole world were copied with a marvellous fidelity; but the inspiration was lacking, the effect was unmoving.

Virtuosity had always been the danger of the Italian school. The rapid degeneration of the ballet was due to the insistence upon a merely technical accomplishment at the expense of grace and spontaneity. Admiration was centred exclusively in the difficulty of the execution of the steps. The most elaborate gestures and evolutions of the old school were laboured and exaggerated. In particular the *pointes* or dance upon the tips of the toes came to be regarded as the highest form of accomplishment. This step when it is abused becomes the curse of ballet-dancing. There are moments when it completes an attitude, giving a suggestion of ethereal lightness, the poise of a winged god alighting for an instant upon the earth. In one brief passage across the stage, the tips of the toes scarcely brushing the dust off the boards, the dancer may capture something of the grace of a bird's flight. But the step in itself is unnatural, and naturalness is above all things essential in the dance. When the part which it plays in the ballet is no longer incidental —the emphasis given to a moment's pose or the suggestion of intriguing daintiness added to a brief passage—but becomes the basis of all the dancer's movements, it results in producing a sense of utter weariness on the part of the spectator. The effect of fairy lightness for which it was originally introduced is lost in the ugliness of the effort. In the music-hall it is not infrequently applauded as though it were the climax of the performance, but the dancer should remember that the same applause has probably a few minutes before been given to a dog walking on its hind-legs. In all arts, and in none more than in dancing, it is always the *tour de force* rather than the nuance of beauty that creates the delight of the crowd.

It was this step which began to take a disproportionate place in the ballet when it entered upon its period of decline. It was a feat which Taglioni could do extremely well, but she never once sacrificed gracefulness to obtain her effect. Her followers on the other hand threw all gracefulness to the winds. They pirouetted, they walked, they tottered on one toe until the shape of their legs became positively disfigured. The popular caricature of the ballet-dancer of the day represented her with her calves standing out like the biceps of a blacksmith. It was a performance which had nothing to recommend it but its painfulness. Little wonder that the public wearied of this meaningless dexterity and came to regard the ballet as but a little above the display of the contortionist.

The final blow to the waning popularity of the operatic ballet was given by the music-dramas of Wagner and Berlioz. Before their advent, a visit to the opera meant primarily a visit to the ballet. Madame Malibran was perhaps the only singer who was able to draw the attention of the amusement-loving world from the fascination of the dance. She alone used to fill the old King's Theatre in London to its utmost capacity on those nights when the ballet was billed as the principal attraction. During the years when Marie Taglioni, Fanny Elssler, Fanny Cerito, Carlotta Grisi, Lucille Grahn, and one or two other of the great *premières danseuses* , were the popular enchantresses, the public turned a deaf ear to the singer. During the vocal and dramatic portions of the opera, the spectators were wont to pass the time in chatting with their friends or promenading in the foyer, until the moment arrived when the *corps de ballet* appeared and riveted their attention upon the stage.

With the début of Jenny Lind the glory of the singing voice once more came into its own. The ballet, which for so long had held the principal place upon the programme, was gradually relegated to an inferior position. At Her Majesty's Theatre it was eventually omitted altogether. At Covent Garden, where the Italian opera found a home in London, it no longer formed a part of the current repertory. Dancers with a certain Continental reputation used to visit England from time to time, but they disappeared almost as silently as they came. The *corps de ballet* , which had been accustomed to give itself amazing airs and to look upon the vocalists, however proficient, as merely interludes in the major attraction of the ballet, was suddenly dispersed. With its proverbial fickleness, the public forgot its old favourites and turned its back upon the dancers over whom it once used to shout itself hoarse. Nobody talked any more about dancing—it was no longer the vogue. Jenny Lind, Titiens, Patti, took the place of Taglioni, Elssler, Grisi, in the popular affection. In Paris, in Milan, and in most of the Continental opera houses, the *corps de ballet* still retained a prominent place upon the programme, but none of the schools succeeded in producing a dancer of the very first order. The dance suffered eclipse. As Taglioni herself remarked, "La danse est comme la Turquie—bien malade."

It is interesting to observe that Wagner in his early days attached no little importance to the ballet in opera. He was disappointed at not being able to carry out his original intention of introducing into *Rienzi* the story of the rape of Lucrece and the expulsion of the Tarquins from Rome in the form of a ballet. He intended the ballet in the Venusberg scene in *Tannhaüser* to be something more that a mere interlude and to have a serious interest of its own. "I have in my mind," he wrote, "an epitome of everything the highest dancing and mimic art can offer, a wild yet seductive chaos of movement and grouping." The argument of this wild scene was set forth at considerable length in the score, but it failed of realisation on the stage on account of the exigencies of the production. When Wagner explained to the *maître de ballet* of the Paris Opera House that the conventional ballet steps would not be in accord with his music, and asked him to supply something "bold and savagely sublime," the ballet-master replied: "I see what you want, but it would need a corps of first dancers." It was in some measure owing to his determination to make the ballet an integral part of the opera that he wrecked his chances of success in Paris. At that period it was customary for the ballet to be performed at an hour sufficiently late in the evening to allow time for the latest patrons of the opera to get to their places. Its inclusion in the first act aroused the wrath of Parisian society, and of the influential members of the French Jockey Club in particular. In later days Wagner wrote of the "fripperies of opera and ballet." Perhaps he would have allowed the ballet a more serious importance if he could have seen the Russian dancers in *Prince Igor*, a performance which must have realised his ideal of a dance "bold and savagely sublime."

Le Corsair may be considered as the last of the cycle of the grand ballets. Rosati, the last of the great *danseuses* , took the part of Medora. An immense sum was expended upon it, but in spite of the splendour of the production it was a failure. The tide had already turned. Only twice after the fifties did London see anything like a revival of the former splendours of the ballet. The dancing of Madame Dore in *Babil and Bijou* at Covent Garden in 1872 achieved the distinction of calling forth an enthusiastic article in *The Spectator* , but the unusualness of such a notice only served to show how completely the ballet had ceased to be regarded as a serious art-form. Shortly afterwards, Marenco, the Italian *maître de ballet* , produced *Excelsior* . After having been played with enormous success in Italy, it was seen in Paris and New York, and finally appeared in England at Her Majesty's in 1885. It had an allegorical meaning agreeable to the spirit of the time, representing the conflict between progress and superstition, invention and reaction. It took a place apart from all contemporary ballets, not so much because of the dancing of individuals—Adelina Rossi was the *prima ballerina* —as on account of the artistry of its design, the beauty of the general movement, the ingenious handling of crowds.

In the seventies the ballet entered into a new phase of life, or, as some would say, decline. Ejected from the opera house, it found a refuge in the theatres of varieties that were then coming into existence. Naturally it changed its character not a little when it left Covent Garden and entered Leicester Square. Twenty-five or thirty years ago, if one went to the Empire or the Alhambra, the Oxford or the Pavilion, one did not choose to have it known. The music-hall was not a proper subject of conversation at the dinner-table or the tea-party. No respectable British matron would have dreamed of being seen within its walls, much less of taking her daughters there. The most expensive seats in the Alhambra in those days, it should be remembered, were three shillings. It was largely owing to the ballet, however, that these houses were lifted into another atmosphere and began to attract a class of audience that would never have entered Leicester Square to see a variety show.

The ballet at the theatre of varieties was a *divertissement* rather than a *ballet d'action* , but nevertheless it was not without considerable merits. The ballets were arranged by mistresses and masters of the dance, like Katti Lanner, Carlo Coppi, Bertrand and Dewinne, who possessed a correct if not a liberal notion of their science; the music was often by distinguished composers, such as Hervé, Sullivan, Jacobi and Wenzel; and at the Alhambra there was an orchestra trained to understand and interpret ballet music. If the *corps de ballet* was lacking in finish, the dancing of the *prime ballerine* , almost all of whom were foreign, left little to be desired. The names of Pertoldi, Gellert, Palladino, Cerali, Giuri, Legnano and Lydia Nelidova are nowadays doubtless well-nigh forgotten, but although they rank below the great names of the preceding generation they were all dancers of distinction.

Indeed the decline of the ballet during this period was due less to the quality of the dancing than to the fact that it was no longer regarded as a serious art-form. The ballet is in effect the combination of a number of arts, co-operating in the production of a single whole. It achieves distinction only when it attracts to itself the best artistic talent of the day. The ballet-master is powerless unless he is assisted by the artist and the musician. The dancing, the music, and the *décor* should be informed by a single spirit. There had been a time when the foremost men of letters and composers had shared in the production of the ballet. Now its direction was left to the music-hall manager. The result was necessarily a vulgarisation of the ballet. It ceased to have any relation to contemporary culture. It became an affair of pretty faces, banal attitudes, waving drapery, tawdry brocades, limelight effects and romping music. It tended to become of the same order as the Christmas pantomime.

But the first reform that was needed was a more serious study of the dancing itself, for the ballet, however interesting the music and the scenery, is essentially an exhibition of the dance. The ballet in England has always suffered from the absence of any official school of dancing. In France, in Italy, in Russia, in Denmark, the academies are maintained by the State; the dancers are in a manner civil servants, holding a permanent appointment and receiving a pension on retirement. An adequate training is therefore possible, a continuous tradition is maintained and a high average, at all events in the technique of the dance, is ensured. In England, however, it has been rather the custom for the *danseuse* to go to this or that teacher to learn a single dance necessary for a certain performance, but not to learn dancing. Indeed it is impossible as a general rule for the dancer out of her slender salary to pay one or two guineas an hour, or whatever the fee may be, in order to attain a proficiency which even when acquired is rarely appreciated. The managers, rightly or wrongly, believed that the public did not care to see good dancing, but only good looks and a dazzling show. The sounder view was probably that taken by the Rev. Stewart Headlam, who always held that the ballet was worthy of serious criticism. Writing in the *Pall Mall Gazette* in 1886 he said: "If either of those houses [the Alhambra and the Empire] want a really new sensation, to take the town, let them have a small ballet, not only with the best principals who can be got—these indeed they have often now—but with the whole ballet composed solely of dancers, picked dancers, who have been regularly and constantly at practice under a really good master." Time has justified his words, for it is in no small degree to this minute and general excellence that the success of the Russian ballet is due.

The ballet, at the time of which we are speaking, had indeed become involved in a vicious circle. Because of its vulgarisation it had fallen into disrepute, and because of its disrepute it was considered demeaning for any serious person to undertake that criticism which was a necessary condition of its reform. In those days it required a certain amount of courage to treat the ballet as worthy of serious consideration and encouragement. The Rev. Stewart Headlam was almost alone in maintaining that the ballet should rank as art and stage-dancing as an honourable profession, and that the religious world had done grievous harm by adopting a policy of isolation towards it. His praise of the ballet of *Yolande* , probably the most beautiful that ever appeared upon the Alhambra stage, drew down the Episcopal censure. It is almost impossible to believe in these days that the Bishop of London should have "prayed that he might not have to meet before the Judgment-seat those whom his encouragement first led to places where they lost the blush of shame and took the first downward step to vice and misery." Mr Headlam's reply was to recommend the Bishop to go to see the *Swans* at the Alhambra or *Excelsior* at Her Majesty's—on the principle that only by the patient study of any form of art can even a bishop understand its laws and intention.

As late as twenty years ago Leicester Square produced some ballets of real excellence. Two in particular, *The Swans* and *The Seasons* at the Alhambra, were exquisite things of their kind. In the latter the dancers were all dressed as birds. The colours were harmonious and restrained and the stage was never overcrowded. But the tendency of the period was to elaborate the staging of the ballet at the expense of the quality of the dancing. The dictatorship of the late Sir Augustus Harris, skilful impresario as he was, led to the overcrowding of the stage, to the accumulation of mere monstrosities of scenery, of costume and of properties. The ballet became a spectacle. It was buried beneath a mass of unmeaning accessories.

The stage was encumbered with gorgeous properties and with the crowd of those who did not dance but merely took their place in the pageant. The effect may have been magnificent, but it was not art. At the same time the ballet-dancers, whose business was to dance, were transformed into members of a chorus, whose chief function was to look pretty. They marched and counter-marched across the stage, performing a number of evolutions with a kind of military precision. Little more skill was demanded of them than of the banner-bearers at a Christmas pantomime. The ballet of the period has been described as chiefly a procession of "rank after rank and file after file of honest bread-winners from Camberwell and Peckham Rye, performing mechanical manœuvres with the dogged perseverance of a company of Boy Scouts." It was, in fact, the honest British bread-winners of the *corps de ballet* , willing but unskilled, that persuaded the British public that ballet was a bore. The result was that popular enthusiasm was directed towards skirt-dancing, and the art of the ballerina fell into undeserved contempt.

Although practically extinct in England the ballet continued to maintain a healthy, if not a flourishing, existence on the Continent. This was due not only to the fact, of which I have already spoken, that the Continental schools of ballet were attached to the great opera houses and usually subsidised by the Government, but also to a high level of criticism and technical knowledge of the ballet on the part of the general public. The indifference of the British public was at once the cause and the excuse of the indifferent performance of the British ballet. This aspect of the decline of the ballet has been well stated by Mr S. L. Bensusan, whose authority on all that concerns the art of theatrical dancing is supreme.

"Not only are many of the steps that must be studied exceedingly difficult," he says, speaking of the work of the Continental ballerina, "but the dancer who has learnt her work in the schools of Vienna, Milan, Moscow, or Paris knows well enough that should she falter in their execution, she will have no chance at all with the public. In Italy, for example, the audience understands the technical side of a dancer's art just as well as it understands the quality of a singer's voice, or just as well as the patrons of a London music-hall understand the chorus of a comic song.... The dancer who failed in ballet to execute a difficult step with absolute neatness and precision, would find a decidedly unpleasant reception awaiting the end of the movement. Her audience have a standard of judgment and will understand what the movement should have been like. In London, on the other hand, several great dancers have told me that it is not worth their while to take trouble about very difficult steps, because unfortunately they are not understood; while something that is obvious and childlike in its simplicity, like a *pas de bourrée*, is safe to meet with a measure of applause at least as great as that which rewards some movements which can only be acquired at the end of long years of study by a very few dancers whose natural gifts are exceptional. If you watch a really distinguished dancer, you are bound to notice that she never has an ungraceful movement or unhappy pose. It is not a case of occasional happy moments, but of one long succession of movements whose rhythm has the beauty of fine verse. The results that make the great dancers so much admired by those who are at any pains to study their work, are quite within the reach of English girls; but it is an unfortunate fact, for which every great ballet-mistress will vouch, that English girls as a class do not take the trouble to work hard enough to acquire the perfect control over limbs and movement that is the reward of their Continental sisters. It is on this account that what is sometimes called English dancing cannot be taken seriously. Of course one cannot blame the English dancers altogether: it is of very little use to prepare a delicate dish for the delectation of the sturdy animal whose favourite food is thistles; and

Danseuses en Scène

FROM A PAINTING BY DÉGAS

while the public remain content with a pretty face, a pleasing figure, a dainty dress, and an air for which barrel-organs cry aloud, English girls may regard it as a labour lost to give them anything better. And yet the successes in years past of dancers like Katti Lanner and Malvina Cavallazzi, and the triumph that has fallen to Adeline Genée to-day, must prove that there is an English audience for better things. Perhaps, if we had more dancers who could and would take their work seriously, the tone of what so many people are generously pleased to call their taste might cease to be contemptible."

CHAPTER V

THE SKIRT DANCE

T HE discovery of a new medium has not infrequently infused a new vitality into a declining art. Certainly the nature of the medium has been almost as important a factor in determining style as the nature of the artist. One of the media through which the dance expresses itself is costume. It has been pointed out how the evolution of the *caleçon* revolutionised the technique of the ballet. The rediscovery of the flowing skirt brought about a revolution in modern dancing.

The flowing skirt appears to us to be a natural appurtenance of the dance. But it must be remembered that the infinitesimal skirt of the ballet-dancer had become a cherished convention, and such is the tyranny of convention that it makes whatever is contrary to it appear to be unnatural. The development of the ballet had been largely due to the abandonment of the fulsome skirt of the early eighteenth century; it was felt that to adopt it once again would be to involve the dance in the swaddling-clothes of its infancy.

The introduction of the long skirt, however, provided an outlet from the impasse into which dancing had been driven. On the one hand was the classical school of the ballet, now in an unfortunate condition of decadence. It lacked all those elements which make of the ballet a living art. The public was sick and tired of it. On the other hand a more or less vulgar type of dancing, which had no relation to art, enjoyed a certain popularity on the music-hall stage. It consisted chiefly of the Clog Dance, believed originally to have come from the cotton mills of Lancashire, and various kinds of acrobatic dancing. In the race for popularity the ugly but energetic Step Dance was first, the classical ballet nowhere. Between the two there was no happy medium.

The Skirt Dance was essentially a compromise between the academical method of the ballet and the grotesque step-dancing which appealed to the popular taste of the time. It stood nearer perhaps to the more serious form of dancing, for in its elements, at least, it was modelled upon the method of the ballet. The exchange, the pirouette, the balance, all the first steps necessary to the ballet-dancer, are the same in both. But while retaining the academical steps as a foundation, it permitted the performer greater license in the use of them. Remembering the passionate dancing of Fanny Elssler, it would perhaps not be correct to say that it introduced more spirit into the dance; but its tendency was towards greater vividness and the play of temperament. The domination of the ballet had in some measure confined dancing to one particular method and, especially in the period of its decline, had exalted technical proficiency at the expense of the display of personality. The Skirt Dance broadened the scope of dancing. In itself never a performance of very great artistic merit, it had all the value of a revolt. It broke down the dominion of a tradition which had become too narrow. It opened up new vistas. It contained the seeds of future movements. In particular it recalled the forgotten dances of antiquity. Though essentially modern, and notably so in its lapses into vulgarity, it nevertheless suggested new possibilities in the grace of flowing drapery, the value of line, the simplicity and naturalness that were characteristic of Greek dance.

But the Skirt Dance was chiefly justified by its success, which can only be described as sensational. The utter absence of enthusiasm for the academic dance made it manifest that the time was ripe for the discovery of a new form of dancing. The wit to invent the novel mode that was to revolutionise theatrical dancing in England came from Mr John D'Auban, for many years ballet-master and director of the dances at Drury Lane. It was of him that "Punch" wrote the doggerel eulogy:

KATE VAUGHAN

Photograph: W. & D. Downey

> "Mr Johnny D'Auban,
> He's so quick and nimble
> He'd dance on a thimble—
> He's more like an elf than a man."

In a short sketch with the unpromising title, *Ain't she very shy?* in which he appeared with his sister, he first introduced the Skirt Dance to the public.

Perhaps the fortune of the Skirt Dance would have been different if it had not at once found an exponent who has no small claim to rank with the great dancers of the century. This was Kate Vaughan. She alone in the host of dancers who obtained a passing fame in this style of dancing possessed a touch of real genius. The fact that she satisfied the discriminating taste of two men of such artistic perception as Ruskin and Burne-Jones is enough to establish her reputation. Burne-Jones called her "Miriam Ariadne Salome Vaughan," and his wife in her biography of her husband relates how he and Ruskin "fell into each other's arms in rapture upon accidentally discovering that they both adored her."

Kate Vaughan was the daughter of a musician named Candelon, who earned a meagre living by playing in the orchestra of the once famous Grecian Theatre. At the Grecian she studied dancing under Mrs Conquest, and it is significant that, unlike most other skirt-dancers, she was thoroughly grounded in the careful method of the ballet. One of her first successes as a dancer was in the *Ballet of the Furies* at the old Holborn Amphitheatre in 1873. Dressed in a black skirt profusely trimmed with gold, she created a great sensation in the rôle of the Spirit of Darkness. After the contortions of the gymnastic dancers, whose popularity testifies to the lamentable condition of the dance at this time—the name of one of the favourites, "Wiry Sal," is a sufficient commentary upon the school!—the exquisite grace of the new dancer, whose style was both precise and refined, was no less than a revelation.

The old Gaiety Theatre was at this time just entering upon its career of phenomenal popularity, and its ingenious manager, Mr John Hollingshead, was not slow to perceive that the new dance would quickly oust the step-dancer and the contortionist from their place in the popular favour. He was among the first to recognise the genius of Kate Vaughan, and he had the means of presenting her to the public to the greatest advantage. From the day in which she appeared in the famous Gaiety Quartet, in *Little Don Caesar de Bazan* , her success was established. She was as supreme in her time as Taglioni, Elssler, Grisi and Cerito had been in theirs. Not only was she the popular idol of her generation, but in spite of the tawdry glitter of the Gaiety stage she was able to engage the interest of serious artists.

Her career is full of pathos if not tragedy. Although she possessed the born instincts of a dancer she had an ambition to excel as an actress. She left the Gaiety and spent most of her life with touring companies. She lived long enough to outstay her welcome. London tired of her; only the provinces remained faithful. Ill-health rendered her performances more and more painful. Her dancing became a torture to her, yet she had the resolution to go through with it even although she frequently had to be carried off the stage for very weakness and pain. Worn out with failure and illness, she left England for South Africa, where she hoped that her fame as a dancer would make her season a success. But her name had no magic for the younger generation that had sprung up in the colony. Neither as a *comédienne* nor as a dancer was she received with any degree of enthusiasm. Almost broken-hearted, she fell ill, and died in great loneliness and distress in Johannesburg in 1903.

In spite of her adoption of a new mode of dancing, Kate Vaughan belonged primarily to the school of Taglioni. Although of course she never reached the perfection of her predecessor, it was to her careful training in the school of the ballet that she owed the ease and grace of her movements and the wonderful effect of spontaneity with which she accomplished even the most difficult steps. She danced not only with her feet, but with every limb of her frail body. She depended not merely upon the manipulation of the skirt for her effect, but upon her facility of balance and the skilful use of arms and hands. Her *andante* movements in particular were a glorious union of majesty and grace. It is true that she

KATE VAUGHAN

IN TURKISH COSTUME

Photograph: W. & D. Downey

condescended at times to introduce into her dance some of those
hideous steps which vulgarised the dancing of the period—in particular
that known as the "high kick"; but even this unpleasant step she accomplished with a certain sense of elegance and refinement which disguised
its essential ugliness and suggestion of contortion. She danced with a distinct inspiration, and upon her style was built up all that was best in the
dancing of her time.

The followers of Kate Vaughan were legion. Most of them were not
dancers at all in the proper sense of the word. They devoted themselves
to the Skirt Dance merely because it was the fashion of the hour, but of
every other branch of dancing they were almost wholly ignorant. But
there were three dancers who were something more than imitators of
Kate Vaughan—Letty Lind, Alice Lethbridge and Sylvia Grey. It is notable that all of them were originally trained for the ballet. Alice Lethbridge showed that she was no revolutionary in her view of what she regarded as the foundation of all technical excellence in dancing, when she
said: "As long as dancing continues, the special movements of the older
ballet, its entrechats, pirouettes, and countless other steps, must also exist,
for they are but the great groundwork of it all."

It was she who developed the Skirt Dance by introducing a revolving
motion, to which she gave the rather vague name of the "waltz movement." While dancing the ordinary waltz, she bent her body backwards
until it was almost horizontal, and in this position, still making all the correct steps of the dance, she rotated the body around its own axis and at
the same time described a large circle round the stage. The swaying of the
body in slow time to the rapid movements of the feet and the graceful
waving of the skirts produced a curious and pleasing effect which won

for her an enormous celebrity. Her other most famous performances were her Marionette Dance, her Fire Dance and some clever shadow dances, which depended for their effect chiefly upon the skilful use of reflected lights. Her dancing was characterised by an extreme vivacity, by the lightnings of eye and hand, which were nevertheless always subdued to the rhythm of the music.

Letty Lind was a dancer almost by accident. When still quite unknown she was somewhat embarrassed by having a song given her in one of her plays. She knew the limitations of her voice and asked if she might be allowed to do a dance instead. Her performance was an astonishing success, and from that moment her career was made. She devoted herself to musical comedy, which was then coming into vogue, realising that there is always room on the lighter operatic stage for an actress who is also an accomplished dancer. For some years she was one of the principal "stars" at Daly's Theatre, but her reputation was always based chiefly upon her dancing. As a skirt-dancer she never reached the perfection of Kate Vaughan, but she always showed herself a dainty and finished artist.

The Skirt Dance, with its swift rushes and billowy undulations of flowing drapery, was at most a charming but trivial dance, of no great pretension or particular significance. It demanded only an average ability on the part of the performer, and no previous training in the intricacies of the dance. It came at a time when, apart from the ballet proper, the usual style of dancing was a kind of energetic double-shuffling and step-dance, generally performed by ponderous principal "boys" in vividly-coloured tights. Kate Vaughan brought to it a personality which would have given distinction to a dance far less artistic, and a daintiness of peculiar fascination. If it had followed more closely the Greek models, with which it had some remote connection, it might have evolved into a dance of greater artistic importance; but its development was in the contrary direction. It degenerated into a romp; it lost whatever precision of technique it had once demanded; and as the width of the skirt grew to larger and larger dimensions, the dancer gradually disappeared in the extravagance of her costume.

The original exponents of the Skirt Dance, as we have seen, were ballet-dancers, whose novelty consisted rather in their costume than in their methods. They adapted the steps of the ballet to the new style without great modification. They brought to the dance that culture of the whole body and not merely of the legs, which is proper to the well-trained ballet-dancer as distinguished from the mere step-dancer. But the misfortune of the

ALICE LETHBRIDGE

Skirt Dance was that it afforded a convenient concealment to the incompetent dancer. Less eminent artists were not slow to perceive that the instruction which had failed to give them distinction in the academic style was quite sufficient to make them resplendent as skirt-dancers. There is a menace that always threatens the dance, no less than the theatre, and that is the incursion of the incompetent professional beauty. The generous public is willing to pardon a multitude of sins for the sake of a pretty face. Now was the signal opportunity for the unintelligent beauty to masquerade as a dancer. Amateurs vied with professionals in seeking success in the simple intricacies of the Skirt Dance. By performing it in a London theatre at a charity matinée, the Countess Russell and her sister gave the dance the sanction of the social world. Philanthropy became the hobby of the fashionable skirt-dancer. A wit remarked that "charity uncovered a multitude of shins."

In a criticism of the period, Mr G. Bernard Shaw ridiculed this cult of good looks and incompetence for which the Skirt Dance was responsible. "Thanks to it," he said, "we soon had young ladies carefully trained on an athletic diet of tea, soda-water, rashers, brandy, ice-pudding, champagne and sponge-cake, laboriously hopping and flopping, twirling and staggering, as nuclei for a sort of bouquet of petticoats of many colours, until finally, being quite unable to perform the elementary feat, indispensable to a curtsey, of lowering and raising the body by flexing and straightening the knee, they frankly sat down panting on their heels, and looked piteously at the audience, half begging for an encore, half wondering how they would ever be able to get through one. The public on such occasions behaved with its usual weakness.... It was mean enough to ape a taste for the poor girls' pitiful sham dancing, when it was really gloating over their variegated underclothing. Who has not seen a musical comedy or comic farce interrupted for five minutes, whilst a young woman without muscle or practice enough to stand safely on one foot—one who, after a volley of kicks with the right leg has, on turning to the other side of the stage, had to confess herself ignominiously unable to get beyond a stumble with her left, and, in short, could not, one would think, be mistaken by her most infatuated adorer for anything but an object-lesson in saltatory in-competence—clumsily waves the inevitable petticoats at the public as silken censers of that *odor di femina* which is the real staple of five-sixths of our theatrical commerce?" For his part, he continues, "the young lady who can do no more than the first sufficiently brazen girl in the street could, may shake all the silk at Marshall and Snelgrove's at me in vain."

It was possibly this fatal facility of the Skirt Dance that gave it its un-paralleled vogue. For a time everybody skirt-danced. There has probably been no such sudden craze for any style of dancing as that which seized England at the time of the famous *Pas de Quatre* in *Faust up to Date* . The schottische-like melody composed for the dance by Meyer Lutz, the Gai-ety conductor, was performed to satiety upon every orchestra in the country. In a mild form the dance was introduced into the ball-room, while certainly for years no pantomime was complete without the in-evitable four girls in short accordion-pleated skirts, standing in a row be-hind one another, kicking out first one leg and then the other in time to the jerky music.

The grace of Kate Vaughan had given an extraordinary vitality to the Skirt Dance; her imitators' lack of grace killed it. Because Kate Vaughan danced in the moonlight—or the livid hue which then passed for moon-light on the stage—every dancer had the lights turned down, with a spe-cial ray from the wings upon her whirling petticoats. Moreover the per-formers of the step-dance from the halls, the only dance really popular with the public before this time, took up the new fashion with alacrity and threw into it more than all their ancient energy. The dance became more and more violent. It was burlesqued out of recognition. The prettiness of the Skirt Dance as it was danced by Kate Vaughan perished in the contortions that were introduced from the Moulin Rouge and popularised in England by Lottie Collins.

LETTY LIND
IN A SKIRT DANCE
Photograph: Ellis & Walery

CHAPTER VI

THE SERPENTINE DANCE

A LTHOUGH its origin was in a manner accidental, the Serpentine Dance was a derivation of the Skirt Dance. The accident happened to an American, with whose name it will always remain associated—Loie Fuller. For the matter of that it was an accident which might have happened to any woman at any time, and as a matter of fact it actually befell Lady Emma Hamilton nearly a hundred years earlier. Goethe relates how at the house of the British Ambassador at Caserta he met "a beautiful young Englishwoman, who danced and posed with extraordinary grace." A moment's whim led her to pick up two shawls of varied hues and wave them as she danced. Struck by the brilliant effect of colour, she called to Sir William Hamilton to hold the candles in such a way that the light shone through the gauzy drapery. She did not pursue the discovery any further, however—indeed in the absence of electricity it would have been of little avail if she had. It is improbable that Loie Fuller ever heard of this incident, for the suggestion of the Serpentine Dance came to her quite spontaneously.

Loie Fuller was born in Chicago. It is said that she made her first bow before the public at the immature age of two, and at eleven the elocutionary powers which she displayed in her little temperance lectures had given her fame throughout the state of Illinois as the "Western Temperance Prodigy." The only lessons that she ever received in dancing were given her by a friend who tried to teach her the Highland Fling, but she introduced so many variations of her own that the friend had to abandon the attempt. At Chicago a professional musician was so favourably impressed with her singing that he offered to give her free tuition for two years. As Loie Fuller was gifted with an excellent memory, assiduous in mastering the details of whatever work she was engaged in, always willing to take any part, big or little, that was offered her, it is not surprising that she should early have won for herself a considerable reputation. She travelled with a touring company, playing in both comedy and tragedy. She first appeared in New York in *Jack Sheppard*, in which her salary was seventy-five dollars a week. Shortly afterwards she was in the cast of *Caprice* in London. She returned to America to take part in *Quack M.D.* at the Harlem Opera House. It was while rehearsing for this piece that she received from a young Indian officer, whom she had met in London, a present which was to change her whole career.

One morning a box was delivered at the hotel where she was staying, and on opening it she found that it contained an Eastern robe of fine white silk, the sort that passes through a ring uncreased. The difficulty—not infrequently incidental to presents—was to know what to do with it. To cut it up would have been a desecration. The quality of the texture was so rare that the piece was fine enough for a museum. Yet its excessive length rendered it useless as a dress without mutilation. But no woman, certainly no American woman, could receive such a present without endeavouring to exhaust all its possibilities as wearing apparel. Taking a piece of string, Loie Fuller fastened the material loosely about her. While playfully waving the soft folds of silk in the air she caught sight of herself in a mirror facing the window. At that moment the sun's rays transfigured the dress into a mass of shimmering light. The beams dancing among the transparent folds of the Eastern material gave it an indescribable delicacy. So strange and beautiful was the effect that the dancer stood for hours before the mirror lost in admiration. She tried innumerable variations of pose, and all were delightful. Suddenly while gazing at the floating clouds of sunlit drapery there came a sound of distant music. The melody was one that the dancer knew well, and in step to the music she danced round the room, tossing the light billowy material about her. At that moment the Serpentine Dance was born.

Loie Fuller devoted the next few months to developing the novel effects which she had discovered and to inventing an accompaniment of slow, gliding steps such as would best accord with the involutions of the skirt rising and falling upon the air.

The invention of the Serpentine Dance coincided with the discovery of electricity as a method of lighting the stage. Until that time gas alone had been used. Loie Fuller immediately saw the possibilities of the new scientific illumination, and with the aid of a few friends she devised a means by which the effect of vivid sunshine could be obtained through the use of powerful electric lights placed in front of reflectors. Then various experiments with colour were tried; for the white light of the electricity were substituted different shades of reds, greens, purples, yellows, blues, by the combination of which innumerable and wonderful rainbow-like effects of colour were obtained. Played upon by the multitudinous hues, the diaphanous silk gave an impression of startling originality and beauty. Coming at a time when the artistic lighting of the stage was scarcely studied at all, the riot of colour created a sensation. Nothing like it had been seen before. The old-fashioned limelight, the flickering gas-jets, the smoking red and blue flames dear to the Christmas pantomime, paled before this discovery of science which apparently possessed inexhaustible possibilities as a stage illuminant.

Loie Fuller introduced her new dance with its accessories to the variety stage in the States, where she soon became famous. But it was not until she came to Europe that her performance received its full meed of appreciation, not as a mere raree-show sandwiched in between the turns of acrobats and performing seals, but as a thing of intrinsic beauty. She visited first Germany and then Paris. The Parisians, who have the habit in common with the ancient Athenians of spending their time in nothing else but either to tell or to hear some new thing, welcomed the novelty of her dancing and quickly adopted her as "La Loie." Her début at the Folies Bergère was a triumph. To the accompaniment of the tinkling strains of Gillet's "Loin du Bal"—a melody inevitably associated with Loie Fuller's dancing—the dazzling figure of light suddenly shone out of the gloom of the darkened stage like some mysteriously illuminated flower, fluttering its petals in the breeze. On batons held in each hand were hung yards upon yards of shimmering gossamer fabric. The least movement of the wand sent the airy mass floating in undulating billows and twisting in streaming spirals. And as the multitudinous moving forms succeeded one another, the light from below shifted through all the combinations of the colours of the rainbow. "La Loie" immediately became the rage. The management of the Folies Bergère engaged her for three years at the handsome salary of two hundred pounds a week—an engagement which unfortunately circumstances prevented her from fulfilling. Not unnaturally, therefore, when some time afterwards she revisited America, she was enthusiastically welcomed on the sacred stage of New York's Metropolitan Opera House.

Strict connoisseurs of the dance are disposed to scoff at Loie Fuller's performance, but the fact must not be overlooked that the arrangement of the drapery is not such an easy matter as might be supposed when viewed from the other side of the footlights. When the enormous dimensions of the skirt are taken into account, the achievement of managing it with grace is not altogether to be despised. The strain on the arms is severe. To wave them in such a manner that the folds of the skirt do not become entangled with one another, and that the whole of it is in motion at the same time, is a feat of dexterity difficult of accomplishment. Certainly the crowd of imitators who sought notoriety in this style never achieved the variety and beauty of the effects which "La Loie" obtained. Amateurs who took up the dance in the enthusiasm of the moment gave exhibitions of embarrassed entanglement that provided their audience with a more amusing entertainment than they had anticipated. I have heard of at least one lady, who elected to follow in Loie Fuller's footsteps for the sake of charity, becoming so enveloped in her hundred yards of drapery that she had at last to be carried ignominiously from the stage in the arms

of an attendant and unravelled behind the scenes like a twisted ball of string.

After it was first introduced, the Serpentine Dance underwent much elaboration. Not only were various harmonies of colour thrown upon the dress, but also strange and wonderful patterns of flowers and lace and barbaric designs. The variety of effects thus obtained were endless. At one moment the skirt was a moving wave of rose-pink; the next it had changed to a dark purple on which gleamed golden stars; afterwards it took the design of a Japanese embroidery; and again it became a flame of fire burning in the darkness. And not content with these bewildering displays, some of those whose business it is to refine upon vulgarity devised a startling and terrible novelty—they utilised the dancer as a backcloth and projected upon her photographs of the prominent people of the day!

Among the most famous of Loie Fuller's dances were the Widow Dance, which she danced in a black robe, the Rainbow Dance, the Flower Dance, the Butterfly Dance, the Good-night Dance and the Mirror Dance. In the latter the multiplication of mirrors gave the appearance of eight Loies dancing at the same time, the whole stage being bathed in a flood of light and filled with a maze of cloud-like vestures. But the most successful elaboration of the Serpentine Dance was that known as the "Danse du Feu." It is said to have owed its birth to another happy accident. It was originally designed for Loie Fuller's play *Salomé* , in which it was the dance commanded by Herod. It was called "The Salute of the Sun," as it drew its inspiration from the effects of the sunset. The Paris audience, however, mistook its intention. Overlooking the evening light which gilded the pinnacles of Solomon's temple, they saw only the fiery rays playing upon the dancer's dress, and exclaimed with delight, "A fire dance, a fire dance!" With her fertile imagination La Loie saw the possibility of the new idea and determined to give them a fire dance indeed.

As in all other Serpentine variations, the Fire Dance necessitated a vast paraphernalia of accessories and an army of associates. The dancer's dress was a voluminous smoke-coloured skirt, to which long strips of the same material were loosely attached. She danced in the centre of a darkened stage before an opening in the floor through which a powerful electric light shot up flame-coloured rays. At first only a pale indecisive bluish flame appeared in the midst of the surrounding darkness; little by little it took shape, quickened into life, trembled, grew, mounted upwards, until it embraced all the stage in its wings of fire, developed into a mighty whirlwind in the midst of which emerged a woman's head, smiling, enigmatical, while a shifting phosphorescence played over the body that the lambent flames held in their embrace. The effect has been described as a superhuman vision. Undoubtedly from the point of view of sensationalism, "La Danse du Feu" was little short of an inspiration.

The Fire Dance became popular. The stages of all the variety theatres in Paris became enveloped in flame. Legions of dancers waving burning veils, under a cross-fire from masked batteries of limelight men, took possession of the stage. The art of dancing appeared about to perish in a general conflagration. Ballets were converted into luminous symphonies. Such themes as *Les Amours du Roi des Ténèbres pour l'Aurore* and *Arc-en-ciel* gave marvellous scope for the display of the talents, if not of the dancers, at any rate of the electricians. The common light of day was henceforth too meagre to please; every atmospheric effect from dawn to sunset was exhausted; moonlight was turned on in floods and the night skies were ransacked for comets and meteors; the kingdom of faery was invaded and despoiled of its sheen by intrepid managers, who poured upon the stage from electric projectors the light that never was on land or sea.

It is doubtful whether this invention of Loie Fuller comes within the sphere of dancing in the proper sense of the word at all. The Serpentine Dance has no steps, no gestures, no poses, none of the usual criteria by which dancing can be judged. The function of the limbs is merely to put measureless lengths of drapery in motion. The dancer juggles with stuffs and veils as others with knives and billiard balls. Loie Fuller's chief merit was her faculty of invention. The best part of her work was done off the stage. When the dance began it was the activity of the army of operators in the wings that became the centre of interest. If we were adequately to discuss the theory of the Serpentine Dance we should have to converse of electricity and optics. It belongs to the realm of science rather than of art. It is an art of electricians and mechanics; it is they, and not the lady upon whom they operate, who should come before the footlights to take the applause and receive the floral tributes of the audience.

Although Loie Fuller was an expert in the art of theatrical illumination rather than in that of dancing, that she possessed a considerable artistic talent is unquestionable. Her love of colour amounted to a real passion. She was peculiarly sensitive to its effects. Every colour had a different influence upon her; she was unable to dance the same measure in a yellow light as in a blue. There was something more than sensationalism in her wonderful Lily Dance, when she disposed the serpentine skirt in such a way that it floated across the stage like the bizarre and gigantic flower of a strange dream; in her Rose Dance, when she sank down covered with crimson petals; in her Radium Dance, one of the most beautiful effects of colour and lighting ever seen upon the stage, almost prohibitive on account of its costliness; in her Fire Dance, which was full of a kind of demoniacal splendour, the madness of a hashish-begotten delirium.

She owed her success very largely to her immense capacity for taking pains. No detail was too small to demand her attention. She had miniature models of the stage constructed for her, with which she conducted her experiments. The complicated lighting apparatus was managed by her brothers, with whom she practised almost daily, inventing and elaborating new effects. She devised with equal care the design of her dresses. The secret of their shape was jealously guarded. On leaving the theatre, her mother, who always accompanied her, enveloped her in a huge black cloak. One silk gown was painted by artists in sections, and the artists themselves had no idea as to what their work was intended for.

Loie Fuller herself is perfectly aware of the limitations of her dancing. She has made her genial apologia as follows:—"To-day everything is governed by laws and precedents, and as I obey no laws of the dancing schools and follow no precedents, I suppose, you know, that really I am not a dancer at all! I have never studied, and I don't believe the ancient Greek dancers ever studied how to move their feet, but danced with their whole bodies—with their head and arms and trunk and feet. I believe that they studied more the *impression* that they wished to convey by their dancing than the actual way of dancing." The criticism that she ignored the obvious fact that no human being was really necessary in her performance at all, and that a small motor or gas-engine could have done the work with equal animation and less fatigue, is a little less than just.

Latterly La Loie has come under the influence of Miss Isadora Duncan. In Paris she directs a school of young children, whom she instructs in the "natural" style of dancing. Her pupils appeared in London in 1908, when they performed Mozart's ballet, *Les Petits Riens* . The performance was no less notable for its lighting than for its grace of movement, as each of the fourteen movements of the ballet was seen against a great open sky, changing with the history of the day from dawn to sunset.

The influence of Loie Fuller upon the theatre will always be felt, particularly in the lighting of the scene and in the disposition of draperies.

But she was never a great dancer. She was an apparition.

92

CHAPTER VII

THE HIGH KICKERS

I T is always interesting to observe the interaction of life and art. All art is of its time, the greatest as well as the least. It may be supposed that the dance has too slight a content to express to be under the obligation of borrowing anything from the ideas of the age. But it has always responded not only to the rhythm of personal emotional life, but also to the larger social rhythm of the time. We have hinted at a relation between the conventional ballets of the forties, with their tranquil emotions, and the placid, domestic temper of the early Victorian era, between the passionate style of Elssler and the spirit of the Romantics. As the century waned, the older formal and unhasting rhythms tended to break up; the pace quickened; the tranquillity which the nineteenth century had carried over from the eighteenth disappeared in the excitement of the *fin-de-siècle* spirit. The temperature of the blood was rising towards the fever-point of the "naughty nineties." They were probably much less naughty than they supposed themselves to be, and they had an unfortunate tendency to mistake vulgarity for vice. Something of the change of the social spirit was reflected in the dance.

Paris began to force the pace in the latter days of the Second Empire. It was a somewhat feverish era, electric with the sense of political change and hazardous speculation, echoing with *coups d'état* and *coups de bourse* . Something of the general unrest penetrated the spirit of the dance. It took on a more exciting allure, became more disordered and furious. The quadrille in particular was completely metamorphosed; its elegance was exchanged for violent movements, resembling the oscillations of a drunkard. In the form of the Cancan and the Chahut it was the delight of the *bals publics* of the French capital. Céleste Mogador, Rose Ponpon, Clara Pomaré, with their *beauté de diable* , gave a vogue to the new and more abandoned style of dancing. These stars disappeared after a brief and noisy career, but the dance survived in undiminished vigour. Its two principal strongholds were the Bal Bullier on Mont St Geneviève and the Moulin de la Galette on Montmartre. The transition from Empire to Republic did not have a sobering influence upon the dance, but rather the reverse. Its natural violence was stimulated by the revolutionary excitement. The fury of the barricades animated its gestures. Students and grisettes, inveterate *révolutionaires* , revelled in it as a kind of vague protest against authority, the bourgeoisie, the spirit of order and propriety. Like the impressionism of contemporary painting, it was championed by those who were rather uncertain as to the articles of their artistic faith but had a very strong sense of being "agin the goverment," civil or spiritual. It was an affirmation of revolution.

To the average home-staying Briton of the period, Paris meant Montmartre, and Montmartre meant the Cancan. Even to-day the word conjures up a vision of the old Moulin Rouge, with its sinister, winking lights, its crude sensationalism, its wild fandango of forced hilarity. In this hothouse atmosphere of feverish yet mirthless gaiety, the dance forgot its ancient origin in hushed forest glades and laughing vineyards, forgot its long sojourn in dignified courts, forgot its strict discipline in the academies; it became little more than an appetiser to the feast of debauch. But among the mob of flamboyant bacchanales for whom the dance was merely a means by which they could display their wares to the market, there were one or two dancers with a distinct personality, who gave the *école mont-*

martroise the vitality, if not the dignity, of a kind of art. The chief of these were La Goulue, Grille d'Égout and Nini Patte-en-l'air.

In her private *dossier* La Goulue was known to the State as Louise Weber. She is said to have earned her soubriquet by her gluttony as a child. Doubtless she had the excuse of the stimulus of hunger, for she was the daughter of poor working-class people.

CONNIE GILCHRIST

(THE GOLD GIRL)

From a painting by Whistler

She had, however, all the impertinent charm of the *petite Parisienne* . And, moreover, she had a passion for her métier. Small, fair, intriguing, with delicately rounded limbs, ivory shoulders and a mutinous little head crowned with light gold hair, she startled Paris by her dancing at the Elysée Montmartre. To the abandon of the Cancan she added in her rendering of it novel effects of an audacity that won her immediate fame. She was to the eighties what Mogador and Rose Ponpon were to the sixties. She became a person of note and the spoilt child of the *jeunesse dorée* . The story is told of how she was invited to supper at the Maison d'Or— she was an astonishingly vulgar little being in those days—by a Russian prince. A well-meaning friend, wishing to give her a genial hint to be on her best behaviour, wrote her a note, which was handed to her on a salver by the *mâitre d'hôtel* . She opened it, and with some difficulty spelled out the advice, to the amusement of her host: "Speak very nicely to the Grand-Duke in order to strengthen the Franco-Russian alliance!"

In her dancing there was no order, no method, but a sure sense of rhythm and an ingenuous frankness and gaiety. To grace of movement she made no pretension—the dance was a negation of it. It was a frenzy, a delirium, a contortion. Her legs were agitated like those of a marionette, they pawed the air, jerked out in the manner of a pump-handle, menaced the hats of the spectators. She sought the *geste suspect* with hand, foot, and body, although at the Moulin Rouge she was obliged to cut discreeter capers. Much of her popularity depended upon a purely personal attraction. She had all the fascination of brilliant and irresponsible youth: she was frankly proud of her charms and daring in displaying them.

In personal appearance Grille d'Égout was in every way her opposite. Dark, thin, with no claims to beauty—her upper jaw was prominent, her chin receding—she resembled La Goulue only in her youth, her spirit and her passion for the dance. In her ordinary movements she had a somewhat gauche and embarrassed manner; hers was the type of the unassuming bourgeoise. But at the first sound of the music everything was changed. She launched into the dance with an astonishing assurance, verve and directness of attack. She was more correct than eccentric, gay rather than voluptuous, arresting by gestures that were droll rather than exciting. Her dancing, a *délire des jambes*, gave a suggestion of the antics of the Parisian gamin.

But the most striking personality of all was that of Nini Patte-en-l'air. She was dark as the night, with a strange, mask-like face of deathly pallor, eyes sunk in deep hollows overarched by thick eyebrows, suggestive of Rops' etching of "La Mort qui danse." Her slight body quivered with intensity of life—*la vie à outrance*—as though charged with electric fluid. The rapidity of her movements was dazzling, and every movement was unforeseen, incalculable, and executed without a trace of effort. Five, ten, twenty times her foot flew above her head; then it remained suspended at the level of her face; it twisted, writhed, agitated, as though it possessed a life independent of the leg; it was a prisoner and struggled to escape; the dancer watched its contortions, an amused spectator of its restlessness; at last it was released; it darted to the ground, recovered its strength and resumed its command of the dance. Then, this by-play over, the dancer rested her hand on the arm of a cavalier, and began a wild, grotesque and fantastic career among the spectators. At every step her foot leapt to the ceiling, her head was thrown violently back, her body maintained a difficult equilibrium, her emaciated features shone with a delirious excitement. Twice she made this frenzied revolution of the hall, then, coming to a sudden standstill, her heel slid along the floor and she sank abruptly in a final dislocation, her legs extended horizontally on either side. It was the dance bewitched, bedevilled, a frenzy and agony of movement, without a parallel except in the maniacal contortions of the Aïssaouas or the revolutions of the howling Dervishes.

These dancers had their followers, of whom the names alone survive —Folette, Rayon d'Or, La Soubrette, La Glu, La Cigale. The dance of *école montmartroise* was a variation upon one perpetual theme—the dislocation of the leg. To name the variations is to indicate the bizarre gestures which formed the stock-in-trade of the school—*La Friture* , *Le Port d'Armes* , *La Jambe derrière la tête* , *Le Croisement* —the latter executed by two dancers whose feet touched in mid-air, describing a kind of ogival arch. It is unnecessary to comment upon this style of dancing. In it the search for the sensational, the incredible, the impossible, reached its limit. The aim of the dancer was to escape as far as possible from the grace of natural bodily movement, to caricature the human form, to imitate the convulsions of the epileptic. It was an instance of one of those maladies which at times afflict the arts. But it is a disease which cannot recur, for the world, having once seen what the dance can achieve when it loses its sanity, is not likely to wish for a repetition of the spectacle. Montmartre remains—chastened, perhaps, if not repentant. It is possible that the tradition still lingers and that there are dancers who, to the confusion of the unsophisticated British or transatlantic stranger, can at need give a dim suggestion of what the *école montmartroise* was at the height, or perhaps rather at the depth, of its fame. But the dance is dead, and not only dead but damned.

England has always kept a circumspect eye upon the heights of Montmartre, and no dance that was danced upon that hill could long be hid. Needless to say, the Cancan in all its native freedom was never performed in this country—for there are performances which depend for their success, if not for their very existence, upon a certain indefinable but quite perceptible *rapport* between performer and spectator, and in England there was no atmosphere for this sympathy to ripen in. But in spite of this, England enjoyed for many years a very sensational imitation of the Montmartre school. The Skirt Dance and the Serpentine Dance, after they had lost the charm of novelty, began to pall. Tired of the monotony of their limited movements, the public was ready to welcome a dance with a wild gaiety and abandon which had all the attractiveness of contrast. The appetite for sensation grows by what it feeds on, and very soon a dancer who could not kick her legs higher than the head, who had not cultivated the "splits" and the "cart-wheel" to perfection, who did not, in fact, exhibit the art of dancing as a series of grotesque contortions, could not count upon holding the attention of an audience. The Cancan was not called by its original name after it had crossed the Channel, nor was it danced as a quadrille; but to all intents and purposes the famous dance which Lottie Collins executed after singing her "Ta-ra-ra-boom-de-ay" song—a dance which sent England and America hysterical with delight—was none other than the famous Cancan, only slightly modified in accordance with Anglo-Saxon traditions of modesty and decorum.

The anglicised version of the Cancan was closely associated with that popular song, the last lamentable echoes of which have only recently died away. The origins of "Ta-ra-ra-boom-de-ay" have been discussed with an interest worthier of a more classical literature. The melody has been derived from an old German Volkslied; it has been asserted that it was heard in a Potsdam tea-garden in 1872 and in a Parisian café a hundred years ago, when it was played as the accompaniment to an Algerian *danse du ventre* ; it is stated to have been whistled and sung for generations among the rice-fields of the Southern States by negroes whose ancestors had danced to it in the barbaric orgies of Central Africa. Whatever its origin, and the latter derivation is the most probable, it was Lottie Collins who first introduced the tune to European audiences. The words, of course, were entirely rewritten, but their barbaric originals could not have been more idiotic than those which were composed to suit the music-hall sense of humour. The dance which accompanied the song was, however, the great feature of the entertainment. Lottie Collins burst upon London just as a dull theatrical season was drawing to a close, and for several years she held the audiences at the Gaiety and Palace Theatre in the hollow of her hand. The rendering of the Cancan on an English stage was a notable event, but Lottie Collins had the invaluable instinct of knowing how far to go without ever once overstepping the border-line of propriety. In spite of the storms of protest which it raised in certain quarters, her dance was never even in its wildest moments very shocking. The extraordinary jerks of her body, her sudden and startling high kicks, her frantic pirouettes, were more astonishing than indecorous; while the spirit with which they were executed and the utter disregard of the sense of rhythm was a revelation to the English public, which was held spellbound.

In America Lottie Collins met with a repetition of her London success. She began her tour with an unfortunate experience. Having to remain in quarantine owing to a case of cholera which had occurred on the voyage, in her exasperation she telegraphed to her manager the concise aspersion,—"Hang America." This indiscretion did not predispose the American people, always sensitive to the appreciation of foreigners, in her favour, and the moment when she made her bow to a New York audience was not unnaturally a critical one. That her subsequent success in the States was as great as it had been in London seems to prove that there was something more attractive in her dance than those who know it only by the melody could have imagined possible. The American idiom lends itself to a description of her performance. "Lottie Collins," so ran the account in the leading daily paper of Kansas City, "has the stage all to herself and she bounces and dances and races all over it in the most reckless and irresponsible way, precisely as if she was a happy child so full of health and spirits that she couldn't keep still if she wanted to. Sometimes she simply runs headlong all the way round the stage, finishing the lap with perhaps a swift whirl or two, or a whisk and a kick. Sometimes she simply jumps or bounces, and sometimes she doubles up like a pen-knife with the suddenness of a spring lock to emphasise the 'Boom.' She is invariably in motion except when she stops to chant the gibberish that passes for verses, but the wonder is that she has breath enough to sing after the first cyclonic interlude." Mr Clement Scott, the dramatic critic, writing of her in the *Daily Telegraph* , confirms the impression of her antics so succinctly conveyed by the Kansas City press. "Bang goes the drum and the quiet, simple-looking, nervous figure is changed into a bacchanalian fury. But wild and wilder as the refrain grows, half-maddened as the dancer seems to become, no one can reasonably detect one trace of vulgarity or immodesty in a single movement."

Undoubtedly popular taste has undergone a radical change within the last generation. The enthusiasm which Lottie Collins aroused is much less intelligible to us now than the homage that in earlier days used to be rendered to Taglioni. Occasionally in the obscurer theatres of the provinces an agile young woman may still be seen throwing out her legs in all directions, performing the "splits" and imitating the rotation of a cart-wheel, but the sight leaves us wondrously cold. We find it difficult to understand how a former generation could have gone delirious with delight over such a display. *Autres temps, autres mœurs.* ...

But lest we should wrap ourselves too closely in our self-complacency we should recollect that, at all events so far as the more popular style of dancing is concerned, we have possibly only exchanged vulgarity for banality. The popular taste is a little more queasy than formerly; it demands not lustiness, but prettiness. Prettiness, insignificant but cheerful, is the peculiar note of the *école anglaise* , if such a thing may be said to exist. Lottie Collins left a legacy of style behind her which her successors possibly found to be a *damnosa hereditas* . But they have prudently selected the prettier features and rejected the rest. The most famous exponents of the English method are the girls who have been trained at the well-known schools of Mr John Tiller, in Manchester, London and Paris. So apt was this training to meet the popular taste that the demand for pupils by theatrical and music-hall managers, not only in England but on the Continent, grew with amazing rapidity. The cry in the world of amusement was for Tiller girls and yet more Tiller girls. It is impossible to mistake a Tiller girl. She is invariably young, invariably pretty, and invariably cheerful, if with a somewhat infantine gaiety; and, while she is free from the affected mannerisms of an inferior ballerina, she is a conscientious performer, with a thorough knowledge of her special though limited technique. She usually appears in troupes of eight or ten. The most famous of these are the Palace Girls, chiefly to be seen at the popular theatre of varieties in Shaftesbury Avenue, London. Others with a marked family likeness, better known perhaps on the Continent than in England, are the Houp-La Girls, the Casino Girls, the Ohio Girls, the Snow Drops, the Cocktails, Les Ping Pongs. No provincial pantomime is quite complete without

REGINA BADET

PREMIÈRE DANSEUSE OF THE PARIS OPERA

Photograph: Central Illustrations

one or other of them. They are to be found in the Parisian Revues, and on the stages of America, Germany, Austria and even Spain, where they are welcomed as the typical representatives of the English school of dancing.

Their charm is of the surface, depending a little upon their science and a great deal upon their maturely immature graces. They go through the same movements in the same manner, at exactly the same time, and with the same unwearying smile. Occasionally they vary the performance with a little singing—simple melodious ditties dealing with bees and honeysuckle, nightingales and the moon, love and the Swiss mountains. But vocal accomplishment is not their strong point. It is not the accent of London or Manchester, but the freshness, the buoyancy, the cheerful innocence, the absence of all excess, the easy execution of simple movements, above all the unimpeachable prettiness, that constitute the chief characteristic of this peculiarly English contribution to the art of the dance.

It may have seemed that in England, at any rate until the recent revival, the dance had fallen quite out of relation to the other arts. It appears to have been familiar only with the music of the streets. It has given no inspiration to sculpture or painting. It has been shamefully cold-shouldered by serious artists. But perhaps it has not been so entirely uninfluenced by popular British art as may seem to be the case. It has certainly worshipped at the same shrine of prettiness and gentle undisturbing emotionalism. It has always been laudably bent on pleasing; it has shunned violence and extremes, even if in so doing it has had to submit to be vapid; it has been artful only in order to appear artless; if never profound it has always been respectable. Surely in their rendering of happy incidents, their genial flow of spirits, their easy and pretty accomplishment, many of the pictures of official British art are inspired by the same spirit as that which animates the Tiller Girls!

CHAPTER VIII

THE REVIVAL OF CLASSICAL DANCING
[1]

W HEN an art grows infirm, there always comes a time when the practitioners hold council over the failing body and prescribe the remedy. And the remedy is always the same—they recommend a return to Nature. Art must go back to its nursing mother, nourish itself again upon the elemental milk from which it drew its earliest life, and be made whole.

Towards the close of the last century, the dance was sick with a fever, sick unto death. The mild and genial palliatives of Mr John Tiller were unavailing. In vain he taught his pupils to smile, to shun the movements of delirium, to simulate a childish glee, to be cheerful even though the heavens should fall. The result too often showed that a dancer might smile and smile and be a failure. Her naturalness was not really Nature. Her passion for honeysuckle and the mountains was as little sincere as the morning blush upon her cheek. The dance could not be tricked back to health by such artless deceptions. It demanded the more radical cure of a genuine return to nature.

The goal was clear, but the way was not plain to be seen. For where was nature to be found? All dancing is merely a refinement upon unconscious bodily gesture. It is the poetic rendering of the prose of ordinary human movement. But the modern world has lost the old graceful motions natural to man in a less artificial state. The characteristic of natural movement is undulation. Waters, winds, trees, all living forms, obey a sovereign law of rhythm. Nature moves in curves and gradations rather than by leaps and bounds. And man in his happiest circumstances—when he lives close to nature, when his occupations are genial and not arduous, when the processes of his labour are even and uncomplicated, when his body is freely exercised and is not forced to conform itself to a special and restricted task—moves with the regular rhythm, the freedom, the equipoise, of nature itself. In that pleasant tract of life, midway between the savage and the civilised state, the occupations of man seem to have developed equally his vigour and his grace. The ancient world had the instinct to know how far labour might be saved without the labourer being sacrificed to the machine. The pause and ictus of the scythe, the even swing of the oar, the circular sweep of the sling, the balance of the seat upon the unbitted and barebacked horse—such were the movements that formed a breed of men capable of all the heights and depths of human grace. Civilisation—in the canting sense of the word—means specialisation of employment, and such specialisation in its turn too often means the deformation of the body. In the modern civilised world the body is usually exercised either too little or too continuously in a single occupation. The dependence upon easy means of locomotion, the resort to labour-saving appliances, the endless dull circulation through the rigid streets, the long periods of inaction interrupted by sudden spells of haste, have quenched the old buoyant and even rhythms. Human motion nowadays tends to be not flowing but angular, jerky, abrupt, disjointed, full of gestures not flowing imperceptibly one into another, but broken off midway. A return to nature means a turning away from the precedents of art to the incidents of contemporary life. The difficulty of applying this precept to the dance lay in the fact that there was no nature to return to, or rather that nature itself had become corrupt and sophisticated.

In this predicament what was to be done? Happily when nature fails us we can still have recourse to a counsellor of almost equal authority and wisdom—the art of the antique world. And whereas for some of the modern arts—for painting and music, for example—classical art is but a taciturn guide, for the dance it is full of instruction. Their interests are one and the same—the body and bodily movement. Greek sculpture has caught innumerable moments of freely flowing action, at a time when action was probably most pure, removed equally far from the rudeness of the savage and the inexpressiveness of the modern. All its salient gestures of sport and war and of the emotional states are as clear to us as if we had been the contemporaries of Pericles and Pheidias. The Greek frieze has been described as a kind of incomplete cinematographic film of the Greek dance. And the so-called Tanagra figures represent a whole alphabet of the silent plastic speech of everyday life.

To recall the dance to nature by the way of Greek art was the work of an American woman, perhaps the greatest personality who has ever devoted herself to developing the art of the dance, Isadora Duncan. Her interests ranged over a wide field of activities. There was a time when she wished to initiate a reform of human life in its least details of costume, of hygiene, of morals. But gradually she came to concentrate her interest upon the dance. For her the dance is not merely the art which permits the spirit to express itself in movement; it is the base of a whole conception of life, a life flexible, harmonious, natural. In the development of the dance she found herself confronted by the dilemma which has just been alluded to. On the one hand was the limited technique of the ballet, on the other the unnatural contortions of the eccentric school. To return to the unconscious gesture of the people—that is to say, the crude, stereotyped gestures of the street—offered no way of escape. She found the solution in a return to the natural gesture of human life as represented in Greek art.

In order to get at her point of view it is best to let her speak in her own words—although, as she would say, one speaks better about the dance in dancing than in commentaries and explanations.

"To seek in nature the fairest forms and to find the movement which expresses the soul of these forms—this is the art of the dancer. It is from nature alone that the dancer must draw his inspirations, in the same manner as the sculptor, with whom he has so many affinities. Rodin has said: 'To produce good sculpture it is not necessary to copy the works of antiquity; it is necessary first of all to regard the works of nature, and to see in those of the classics only the method by which they have interpreted nature.' Rodin is right; and in my art I have by no means copied, as has been supposed, the figures of Greek vases, friezes and paintings. From them I have learned to regard nature, and when certain of my movements recall the gestures that are seen in works of art, it is only because, like them, they are drawn from the grand natural source.

"My inspiration has been drawn from trees, from waves, from clouds, from the sympathies that exist between passion and the storm, between gentleness and the soft breeze, and the like, and I always endeavour to put into my movements a little of that divine continuity which gives to the whole of nature its beauty and its life."

It must not be supposed that Isadora Duncan despised technique or attempted to dispense with it. It was the technique of the current modes of dancing that she found unsatisfactory. "I have closely studied the figured documents of all ages and of all the great masters," she says, "but I have never seen in them any representations of human beings walking on the extremity of the toes or raising the leg higher than the head. These ugly and false positions in no way express that state of unconscious dionysiac delirium which is necessary to the dancer. Moreover move-

ments, just like harmonies in music, are not invented; they are discovered."

It is a mistake, which some exponents of the "natural" style of dancing have fallen into, to imagine that they can express the spirit that moves
them by any haphazard agitation of the limbs. To dance "naturally" does
not mean to dance impromptu, relying upon the inspiration of the moment. In art the simplest effects are usually those which have cost the
greatest effort, and no effort is more severe than the attempt to imitate
the inimitable model of nature. The dance demands as rigorous a technique as any other art. Without a technique it is inarticulate. Miss Duncan

ISADORA DUNCAN

has undergone a training as elaborate as any *prima ballerina* . From her childhood upwards she has devoted twenty years to the study of the dance. She had to invent, or rather discover, her own technique. Taking for her models the poses of Greek art, she endeavoured to reconstruct from a single attitude the whole continuous flowing movement, of which the statuesque pose is of course but an arrested moment. She had to fill in the gaps, as it were, in the interrupted cinematographic film, to pass rhythmically from one gesture to the next. She found at first that her body failed to respond. It suffered from the unpliability, the general wrongness of movement, which is the outcome of modern conditions of life and the loss of tradition. She found that she had to begin with the elements of motion, to learn to walk, to run, to leap rhythmically before she could dance rhythmically. She started therefore to learn to govern her body, to recover a lost art of balance and flexibility, to make each slightest movement a harmonious expressive gesture. For she demands none but the finest gestures for the dance. Everything common and contemptible she would exclude by a severe test.

"Every movement that can be danced by the side of the sea without being in harmony with the rhythm of the waves, every movement that can be danced in the midst of a forest without being in harmony with the swaying of the foliage, every movement that can be danced, naked, in the broad sunlight of the open field, without being in harmony with the vibration and solitude of the landscape—all these movements are false movements in that they are discords in the harmony of the great natural lines. That is why the dancer must choose above all the movements which express the strength, the health, the grace, the nobility, the languor or the gravity of living things."

The steps of the dance, therefore, have to be studied with a care which makes even the elaboration of the technique of the ballet appear simple. But the steps are not the end; they are only a means. The end at which in Miss Duncan's view the dance aims is "to express the noblest and most profound sentiments of the human soul, those which come from Apollo, from Pan, from Bacchus and from Aphrodite. To see in it no more than a frivolous or agreeable diversion is to offer an insult to the dance." She is in thorough accord with the Greek view that the dance re-acts upon the moral mood. "The attitudes which we take have an influence upon our soul. A simple throwing back of the head, done passionately, causes us a sudden tremor of joy, of heroism or of desire. All gestures have a moral resonance, and thus can directly express every possible moral state."

Hers also was the Greek view that music and the dance should be mutually interpretative. Before her time music had been regarded primarily as an accompaniment, a time-keeper; she enunciated the theory that its function was to give the keynote of the mood of the dance. Music and the dance were to be two bodies animated by a single soul. She selected as her prime composer Gluck, a master of simple and obvious melody. But she not only interprets him, she enlarges and sublimates him. The handling of musical themes in this way is of course a dangerous matter, and might give rise to discussion which would be out of place in this book. It may be maintained that a consummate composition, a symphonic movement by Beethoven, is complete in itself. The best music is its own interpreter and needs no elucidation. Music, moreover, is large and broad in its emotional expression; it transcends words, and how therefore should it not transcend gesture? It is as likely as not that a choregraphic commentary may limit rather than enhance the musical conception. It is possible that the movements of a dancer might not at all correspond with the mood that a Chopin nocturne, for instance, awakes in us. To these misgivings I do not propose to reply. The only adequate answer is to be found in Miss Duncan's dancing. On this debatable ground her tread is sure. In each of her interpretations of music there is a self-evident rightness which silences censure.

Miss Duncan at first suffered the lot of most reformers. Novelty is usually found to be amusing; the public laughed because it failed to understand. When she appeared some twelve years ago in New York, she had already struggled long and hard to perfect

ISADORA DUNCAN

Photograph: Dover Street Studios, Ltd.

her art and she sorely needed the invaluable stimulus of recognition and appreciation. She performed a dance which was suggested by "The Rubáiyát" of Omar Khayyám. The newspaper humorists made merry over her work. One summed up the general verdict in the phrase: "Our public will probably prefer Omar's lines to Miss Duncan's."

When she came to Europe, however, Miss Duncan's art met with speedy recognition. In rapid succession she captured Berlin, Paris, St Petersburg and London. London perhaps found the new gospel somewhat hard to accept, but the educational authorities both in Germany and France were anxious to obtain her services in the instruction of children. In Paris she has trained a troupe of young children whose delightful dancing charmed London audiences a year or two ago.

In the power of expressing the depth and subtlety of spiritual moods Isadora Duncan is supreme. She is a poet no less than a dancer. Her dancing is so deeply rooted in the soul that it ignores the superficial and often coquettish graces of the popular dancer. And yet she is feminine in her dancing, but feminine in the simple, calm, womanly grandeur of the three fates of the Parthenon marbles. Hers is the essential and eternal type of womanhood, the type of the Madonna, of the peasant woman, breathing of the warm earth and the open air, of Ceres rather than of Circe. Her dance has perhaps the beauty of full summer rather than of spring. Its lines are flowing, but full of dignity and restraint. There is perhaps still a suggestion of the frieze in it. A new technique necessarily at first inclines towards rigidity.

There is no surer proof of the true greatness of her art than the fact that it can produce in the spectator that sense of shock which only work of an elemental character can give, a shock which sends the mind surging forward down vistas opening up an undiscovered prospect not merely of art but of life. This sensation has been well described by Mr W. R. Titterton in a glowing pæan of praise. "I remember when I first saw her, at the Theater des Westens in Berlin. My friends had led me to expect something fine, and then the Duncan came and struck me like a thunderclap. Will you believe me? I shuddered with awe. Once in a century, in ten centuries, comes a New Idea, and here was I the spectator of the latest born. In this idea—this free, simple, happy, expressive rhythmic movement—was focused all I and a hundred others had been dreaming. This was our symbol—the symbol of a new art, a new literature, a new national polity, a new life. I saw crowds of happy children, of happy men and women, dancing that dance on village greens, in the green forest, on the green hill-tops. Pedants at their books, pedants at their figures, pedants on their platforms vanished in smoke before the exultant dances of this glorious woman. As the walls of Jericho before the trump of Joshua, so before her the factory walls fell down, the festering slums and ugly places of London crumbled to dust, and away to Arcady we danced to the sound of her Shepherd's piping."

If Isadora Duncan propounded the gospel of the classical dance, Maud Allan promulgated it with the greatest popular success. She won the ear of England for the new word. Not that she was by any means a mere copyist—her talent was too original for that. Coming after her great predecessor, she nevertheless found her own inspiration in herself. With a certain assurance in the strength of her own individuality, she treated the classical dance with some freedom and boldness. She added the personal touch that gained the applause of the crowd.

Miss Maud Allan is Canadian born, but she spent the best part of her childhood and youth in the state of California. There she lived a breezy out-of-door life, romping, riding, swimming, mountain climbing, drinking in health with the virgin air—all unconsciously, no doubt, acquiring the strength and suppleness of body that were to be invaluable to her in later years. Very early she began the serious study of music, but even in those early days she seems to have been conscious of the possibilities of the expression of emotion through the medium of gesture. When Sarah Bernhardt visited San Francisco, the art of the great actress left a deep impression upon her. Shortly afterwards, when she was playing at the piano, her mind still attentive to the rhythm of the French artist's gestures, her mother asked her of what she was thinking. "Of Sarah Bernhardt's wonderful talent, of the beautiful movements of her body," she replied. "She seems to express more with it than with her lips."

It was decided that Maud Allan should go to Berlin to continue her musical studies at the Royal High School of Music. The next five and a half years of her life were spent in an atmosphere of music, literature and art. Her work was varied by travel in Italy and elsewhere. Her visit to Italy was a turning-point in her artistic career. Already at times she had experienced a feeling of being a prisoner while at the piano; music was still an intense delight to her, but it was no longer all-sufficing. A new idea took shape in her mind as she stood before Botticelli's "Primavera" in Florence, an idea that she too might render her body eloquent to speak of the joy of spring and of the scented woods and of emotions yet more various and profound. She returned to Berlin, where she developed her idea, concentrating her interest on physical culture, studying in museums and libraries the poses of classical art, seeking to discover the relation between music and gesture. The new interest so engrossed her that it allowed no time for any other pursuit. She no longer had any doubt as to her true vocation. She left the Royal High School of Music and began her career as a dancer. She gave her first public performance in Vienna in 1903. Three years had elapsed since the idea had crystallised before Botticelli's picture in Florence—three years of continuous training and preparation.

It is interesting to note that when Joachim saw the dance-programme of his young friend, he called her aside and said: "Little girl, you may dance anything you like, but, dear child, please don't dance my Beethoven!" It was another musician, however, Marcel Remy, the Belgian composer, who gave her the greatest encouragement and assistance in the prosecution of her studies.

The success of the new dancer in Vienna was immediate, and in the following years she appeared in most of the larger cities of Germany, Switzerland, Austria and Hungary. It was in 1907 that she received the command to appear before King Edward VII. at Marienbad. "I remember that it was with fear and trembling that I began my work," so she tells the story, "although when in the midst of any of my dances I am seldom cognisant of any personality near. But I think I should be forgiven if, that once, the thought of England's King watching me gravely influenced me and, afterwards I realised, favourably. I think it was the happiest moment of my life when he took my hand with his calm, great dignity and told me he considered my art a beautiful one, and my dances worthy of the word classical."

In the spring of 1908 Maud Allan first appeared before an English audience at the Palace Theatre, London. Since that date much water has flowed under the bridge, and it is not without interest now to recall the notice that appeared in *The Times* newspaper the following morning: "There is little doubt that Miss Maud Allan will make a great success. If so she will be the first to rouse London to enthusiasm with a kind of dancing to which it has never yet taken very kindly—the dancing of gesture and posture. As Miss Allan represents it, it is a thing of such interest and beauty that it may even drive high kicking off the stage."

The programme informed us in magniloquent phrase that the new dancer had "ransacked the shrines of plastic beauty and worshipped humbly and prayerfully before the Art of the Universe." Little wonder, therefore, that there was a hush of expectancy when the violin bows glided softly into the opening strains of Chopin's valse in A minor and, preceded by a sinuous arm, the dancer slipped through the velvet hangings, drawn forward apparently by the magnetism of the music. Her limbs and feet were bare, her form lightly clothed in a loose classic drapery. A ripple ran along her arms from the shoulder to the finger-tips, undulating like a wave of the sea. When the music changed from the minor to the major key, her body passed into the corresponding mood, suddenly becoming brilliant with hope and delight. Then as quickly the joy faded out of her face and limbs, and she relapsed with the music into a passive despair. When the music ceased, her heart too seemed to have ceased beating. Silently she glided back through the curtain. Already London had capitulated.

Mendelssohn's "Spring Song" was an *allegretto grazioso* chase of

MAUD ALLAN

Photograph: Foulsham & Banfield, Ltd.

butterflies and plucking of wild flowers. With rapid sallies hither and thither, now a-tiptoe, now on bended knee, she danced the joy of all living things in the spring. The dream she dreamed before Botticelli's "Primavera" had become reality. A comparison with Pavlova's "Danse des Papillons" inevitably suggests itself, and it is hardly possible to claim that in sheer brilliance of movement, in papilionaceous gaiety, the "natural" school has yet outstripped a style that is founded upon the older technique of the ballet.

But the climax of the performance was the "Vision of Salomé." Many harsh things have been said of this dance, from the propriety of the costume of jewels and gauze to that of rendering a stage version of a Biblical episode. It has been called by a respectable critic, "sensuous, decadent, *macabre* ." It was stated that it preserved a nice balance between the lascivious and voluptuous. Above all, the Corporation of Manchester, believing that it would sully the immaculate atmosphere of their city, prohibited its performance within the limits of their jurisdiction—an action which resembles nothing so much as that of an English duchess, who, when she was offered the translation of a French play that she was witnessing, refused it, saying, "I do not wish to understand." It is to be feared, however, that the deputation of City Fathers that was sent down to witness the dance was able only to misunderstand. To state that the dance was as pure in intention as it was powerful in execution would be a superfluous commentary. I cannot do better than let the dancer relate in her own words the meaning of the vision:

"Drawn by an irresistible force, Salome in a dream descends the marble steps leading from the bronze doors that she has just flung to, behind her frightened attendants. The sombre stone obelisks, backed by the inky darkness of the cypress trees, shut out the silver rays of the moon, and, save for the flickering red light of the cresset flames that the slaves have lit, all is mystic darkness, and to Salome's overwrought brain all is fantastic, vague.

"She lives again the awful moments of joy and of horror which she has just passed through. Alone in the gloom the poor child's fancy assumes dominion over her.

"Slowly, to the strains of the distant music, reminiscently she raises her willowy arms. The movement thrills her whole slender frame and she glides as if in a dream. A voice whispers 'Your duty—your duty! Does not the child owe obedience to its mother?' On, on—wilder and more reckless than ever before! She sees once more the greedy glittering eyes of her stepfather—she hears again the whispered praises and encouraging words of her mother, and Salome, child that she is, realises a power within her and exults. She sees again her triumph approach, her swaying limbs are in readiness to give way, when suddenly from out of the sombre death-still hall the wail of muffled distress—and a pale, sublime face with its mass of long black hair arises before her—the head of John the Baptist! There is a sudden crash. She is horror-stricken! Suddenly a wild desire takes possession of her. Why, ah! why should her mother have longed for this man's end? Salome feels a strange longing, compelling her once more to hold in her hands this awful reward of her obedience, and slowly, very slowly, and with ecstasy mingled with dread, she seems to grasp the vision of her prize and lay it on the floor before her. Every fibre of her youthful body is quivering; a sensation hitherto utterly unknown to her is awakened, and her soul longs for comfort. Hark! a sound of approaching feet. Frightened lest her treasure be taken from her before she has solved its mystery, she stands guard over it, and when the footsteps die away in the distant halls her relief knows no limit! In the mad whirl of childish joy she is drawn again to dance—dance around this strange silent presence. Soon exhaustion breaks the spell. Salome, Princess of Galilee, lies prone on the cold grey marble.

"The awakening is that of her childish heart. The realisation of a superior power has so taken possession of her that she is spurred on to sacrifice everything even unto herself to conquer. Reared in luxury—her every wish granted since her days began—was it to be thought possible she would subject herself to the will of another, a stronger and an intangible force at that, without a fierce conflict?

"What passes in those few moments through this excited, half-terror-stricken, half-stubborn brain makes of little Salome a woman!

"Now, instead of wanting to conquer, she wants to be conquered,

MAUD ALLAN

craving the spiritual guidance of the man whose wraith is before her; but it remains silent! No word of comfort, not even a sign! Crazed by the rigid stillness, Salome, seeking an understanding, and knowing not how to obtain it, presses her warm, vibrating lips to the cold lifeless ones of the Baptist! In this instant the curtain of darkness that had enveloped her soul falls, the strange grandeur of a power higher than Salome has ever dreamed of beholding becomes visible to her, and her anguish becomes vibrant.

"She begs and prays for mercy of the stern head—alas, without response! Salome flees in despair, and though her pride, her princely rank, confront her, and she halts, it is but for a moment. The Revelation of Something far greater still breaks upon her, and stretching out her trembling arms turns her soul rejoicing towards Salvation. It is gone! Where, oh, where! A sudden wild grief overmasters her, and the fair young Princess, bereft of all her pride, her childish gaiety, and her womanly desire, falls, her hands grasping high above her for her lost redemption, a quivering huddled mass."

It was a dance of a strange and haunting fascination, deriving no little of its disquieting effect from the weird Oriental strains of Strauss's music. There were many who found themselves unaccountably drawn to it and were compelled to return to the tragic vision night after night. Yet as a presentment of tragic emotion, finer even than the "Vision of Salomé," or the rendering of Chopin's "Funeral March," was the dance of "Ase's Death" in Grieg's *Peer Gynt* suite. It was a study of mournful poses, inspired by that grief which lies too deep and still to explode in tumultuous and exciting gesture. There is, however, in her ecstasies both of joy and

grief just that lack of fire which makes intelligible, if it does not quite jus-
tify, the somewhat harsh words of Mr W. R. Titterton when he says of
Miss Maud Allan that "she is the English Miss in art. She is an ineffectual
angel beating in the limelight her luminous wings in vain. She has many
pretty movements; she is light and dainty, she has an elfin prance, with
bent knee and waving hands, but she has no temperament, and no presence; she is spectral; you think you can see through her. And above all,
she is monotonous. She repeats and repeats and repeats. How she sickens
me in the end, for example, with that, at first, so beautiful ripple of the
hands."

The truth may possibly be that that freedom from convention in
which she glories is in reality a bondage. In her own words, "dancing is
the spontaneous expression of the spiritual state." The dance is "not an
acquired but a spontaneous art, revealing the temperament of the
dancer." She is compelled to acknowledge the necessity for technique, but
she fears that if it becomes excessive the art will no longer be able to stir
the soul. In this theory lurks a certain element of danger. The dance, like
all the arts, seeks the effect of spontaneity, of inevitableness, but this
spontaneity is highly self-conscious. And it expresses itself most readily
by technique—for technique, when it is really fluent, does not hinder but
facilitates the expression of temperament. For us moderns the "spontaneous" gesture is the clumsy, inexpressive movement of everyday life; the
dancer requires a conscious technique that comes more naturally to her
than the unconscious technique of the street, in order to be truly spontaneous and expressive. It is perhaps her detestation of the stereotyped
steps of the ballet that causes her to incline to the opposite extreme. But
she herself would be the first to admit that her art has cost her pains no
less than that of the ballet-dancer. It is one of her complaints that many
suppose that she has learned to dance with no more than the exertion of

a fluttering butterfly. It is not for Miss Allan herself, but for her imitators, that the theory that technique is relatively unimportant is so dangerous a pitfall. The conventions of classical or "natural" dancing are not yet so fixed as those of the ballet. Where the path is less clearly marked out there is more danger of going astray. Would-be dancers of the "natural" school, imagining that nothing is so easy as to dance "naturally," forget that they have to unlearn the movements they are accustomed to before they can produce anything worthy of the name of art.

If Isadora Duncan is a poet, Maud Allan is before all things a musician. In the musical qualities of her art she has no rival. Apart from her instinct for music, she has profited by a musical training such as probably no other dancer has been equipped with. Her steps are to the eye the exact equivalent of the notes which reach the ear. One of the most felicitous of her accomplishments is her ability to pass with the music from the major to the minor key, or *vice versa* . When a phrase occurs first in one key and then in the other, it is repeated in her dancing with just that modification of aspect and accent which expresses the change of mood. Some of the movements in Grieg's first *Peer Gynt* suite gave her admirable scope for this beautiful art of transposition. The faithfulness with which her movements follow the moods of the composer is probably only fully realised by those who are musicians as well as connoisseurs of the dance. Her translation of music has not seldom that rare quality of translations of being finer than the original, and there are not a few who, when they hear again, unaccompanied, the music which her dancing has ennobled, will be conscious of a sense of incompleteness and loss.

If only Joachim had seen her art in its maturity, he would perhaps have been content to allow her dance his beloved Beethoven!

In any account of the classical dance it is scarcely possible to forbear mention of Mlle Magdeleine, although it is difficult to know exactly where to place her. For the characteristic of her dancing is that it purports to be unconscious. Some eight or nine years ago Mlle Magdeleine came for hypnotic treatment to Professor Magnin of the Paris School of Magnetism. M. Magnin accidentally discovered that while in a state of trance she was susceptible to the influence of music in a quite extraordinary degree, and that although she had learnt nothing of the art of dancing, she accompanied the music that was played to her in her trance with motions of the utmost beauty and significance. She was strictly examined by a number of eminent scientists, who certified that to the best of their belief her dancing was performed in a genuine state of unconscious, or rather subconscious, activity. She interpreted with strange suggestiveness the music that the foremost musicians of the day played to her, and the painters and sculptors who saw her, including Rodin, were astounded at the strength and beauty of her poses. Naturally the main interest of her performance rests upon its genuineness, and it is easier to believe that it was given under true hypnotic conditions than that the best scientific judgment of the day was deceived.

Mlle Magdeleine interpreted music ranging in character as widely as Handel's "Largo," a valse of Chopin's, and "The Marseillaise." Her rendering of the latter was the very embodiment of human passion and blood-lust. Her power of dramatic expression is indeed terrifying. In her gestures there is at times something tremendous and heroic; at other times they are distinctly faulty and fall into the conventional and the commonplace. It is said that her trance tends to become mixed with the recollections of her waking consciousness, and that when the two states ultimately coincide she will lose her distinctive quality, her absolute rightness of gesture. In any case her dancing is a unique phenomenon; she cannot found a school or perpetuate a method. But she points the way for the art of that great tragic dancer of whom the dance is expectant—an art which was only partially realised in the dancing of Miss Maud Allan. Of the three Ladies of Sorrow of whom De Quincey speaks it was perhaps possible for the dancer of the "Vision of Salomé" to represent our Lady of Tears, "who goes abroad upon the winds when she hears the sobbing of litanies or the thundering of organs," or even of Our Lady of Sighs, "whose eyes are filled with perishing dreams, and with wrecks of forgotten deliriums"; but it was reserved for the Magdeleine to portray that third and most terrible sister, Mater Tenebrarum, Our Lady of Darkness, the defier of God, the mother of lunacies and the suggestress of suicides, who "moves with incalculable motions, bounding and with tiger's leaps," who "wears the fierce light of a blazing misery that rests not for matins or for vespers, for noon of day or noon of night, for ebbing or for flowing tide." The dances of delight and gaiety come almost instinctively to those of a happy temperament; but the dances of grief, of fear, of madness, of despair, these are they which put the dancer to the severest test, which strip her of the acquired graces of the schools, and leave her dependent only on the quality of her own soul.

MAUD ALLAN

IN CHOPIN'S FUNERAL MARCH

Photograph: Foulsham & Banfield, Ltd.

Of the uninspired imitators who have followed in the steps of the great dancers of the classical school, there is happily no need to speak at length. Mme Knipper-Rabeneck of the Artistic Theatre of Moscow trained a group of dancers, who performed in London last year. Their interpretation of the music which they accompanied with their dancing was not very subtle, but if they failed to catch the finest shades of Schumann, Brahms and Chopin, they nevertheless gave a pleasing exhibition of youthful liveliness. The sisters Wiesenthal have added to the classical method a "pretty fluttering, tottering marionette manner of their own." And Lady Constance Stuart Richardson was the first of the aristocratic amateurs who, when any new style of dancing becomes the vogue, are always ready to rush in where professionals sometimes fear to tread.

Indeed there are signs that classical dancing may be overtaken by a fate not unlike that which befell the Skirt Dance—an event which would indeed be a calamity, and not, as in the earlier mode, a happy release. Whatever may be said in dispraise of the school of the ballet—and it has its detractors not a few—it has at least the advantage of possessing a technique, the terrors of which are sufficient to protect it against the incursion of that mob of gentlewomen who dance with ease, or rather who would dance with ease were it not for the necessary pains without which that ease cannot be acquired. "Natural" dancing, by its very name, is inviting to those who are averse to hard work. The theory that a dancer can ignore with impunity the restrictions of technique, that she is bound to please if only she is natural and happy, and allows herself to follow the momentary inspiration of the music, and dances with the same gleeful spontaneity as a child dancing to a barrel-organ, is a doctrine as seductive as it is fatal. Already we have seen upon the stage performers who, in the name of Greek art, race and romp rather than dance. We are threatened with performances in which naïve young creatures in tenuous classic drapery amuse themselves by capering on bare feet, gathering and scattering make-believe roses, splashing in imaginary rivers, undulating snaky arms, shooting arrows, playing ball, butterfly catching. The dance cannot return to nature, in the sense which Isadora Duncan intended, by returning to this rather kindergarten Arcadia. The classical dance has its hidden law, which is perhaps more difficult than that of the ballet because it is more secret. If the dancer despises technique and relies only on her natural endowment, she must at least expect that the least flaw of beauty, grace or intelligence will be exposed in painful nakedness to the general gaze.

CHAPTER IX

THE IMPERIAL RUSSIAN BALLET

I T is now time to pick up the thread of the story of the ballet.

We have seen how a new spirit in dancing came from the West; for the new spirit in ballet we must look to the East. [2] Many strange and fine things of the spiritual order have come out of Russia in these latter times. Our music, our literature, our art, have been profoundly affected by the spirit of that people which appears to have all the unfathomable reservoirs of barbaric life to draw upon. But perhaps there has come to us nothing so supremely excellent, so unsurpassably beautiful, as Russian dancing.

As with all other peoples who still preserve the traditions of the elder generations, with the Russians dancing is a natural act. The peasants learn the graceful national dances, which vary from province to province, as simply as they learn their mother tongue. In summer, on the evenings of Sundays and holidays, the gaily-decked youths and maidens collect in a field or on a bridge near the village and dance to the music of the twittering *balalaika* or the monotonous ululations of a cheap concertina. Unfortunately in Russia, as everywhere else, the old order is giving place to the new, and for the immemorial national dances are being substituted foreign quadrilles and lancers. But though the character of the dance changes, the passion and the natural aptitude for it remain. In the People's Palace at St Petersburg the young men and girls from the factories may be seen dancing the intricate measures of the mazurka with an ease and abandon which some of the trained dancers of Western Europe might envy.

To this native spirit, however, the ballet owes little or nothing. Doubtless it has in a manner fertilised the soil, created a public interested in the dance and, if heredity counts for anything, provided a raw material ready for the ballet-master to mould to his will. But the ballet, as I have said before, is in its origin aristocratic, and nowhere more so than in Russia. The Russian ballet is entirely the product of the Court. It was of course originally a foreign importation. The first ballet was presented in 1675, before the Tsar Alexis, the second of the Romanovs. Peter the Great, in his efforts to westernise Russia, introduced the Western modes of dancing, and, as he was his own shipwright, so he was his own dancing-master. He sets about teaching his Court, and himself made such "caprioles," says Bergholz, that any dancing-master might envy him.

But the institution of the ballet in Russia was due to the Empress Anne. In 1735 she appointed the Neapolitan composer Francesca Areja to compose the music and conduct the orchestra, and a Frenchman, Landé, to act as ballet-master. She commanded an Italian *intermedio* with a ballet to be played before her once a week. At first, as there were yet no professional dancers, the young noblemen of the military cadet schools were instructed in the dance. Gradually they were superseded by a specially trained corps. Landé collected a number of boys and girls of the poorer classes and trained them free of charge. So delighted was the Empress with their performance that she undertook to defray all the expenses of their education out of the Imperial exchequer. Landé received a fee for teaching them, rooms were provided for them in one of the palaces, and we learn that the children were entrusted to the care of a widow of one of the Court coachmen. Such were the modest beginnings of the famous Dramatic School of St Petersburg.

Catherine II. followed in the footsteps of her predecessor. In her reign the services of the cadets were no longer required. To her initiative was due the erection of the Grand Theatre, which is now supplanted by the famous Marianski Theatre. She organised the theatre and brought it into relation with the bureaucratic regime, appointing a director, with two committees under his control, one in Moscow and one in St Petersburg, to superintend theatrical spectacles.

Didelot, who was called to St Petersburg in 1802, raised the ballet to a level of excellence which was not surpassed even in Milan. As a ballet-master he was a martinet, almost a fanatic in his passion for his art. Under him the ballet took that prominent place in Russian life which it has never since lost. He regarded *plastique* and *mime* as even more important features in the ballet than dancing itself. He insisted that there was no limit to what the ballet could express, and to prove his case staged Racine's tragedy, *Phèdre* , in ballet form with considerable success. So great became the popularity of the ballet that even when opera came into fashion it was the custom for the *corps de ballet* to repeat in dumb show during the *entr'actes* the foregoing act of the opera.

During all this time the Imperial Ballet closely followed the academic Italian tradition. It was in no way distinctively Russian. Fifty years ago, and even less, most of the principal dancers in Moscow and St Petersburg were Italians—a complete reversal of the state of affairs at the present day, when Preobrajenskaya, one of the greatest dancers at the Marianski, appears as *prima ballerina* at La Scala, the home of the ballet in Milan.

The excellence of the Russian ballet is the direct outcome of the system of State maintenance and control, which has been in vogue for a century and a half. The large expenditure necessary for its upkeep is met by the funds annually set apart for the Minister of the Court. The Imperial Ballet provides all the dancers for the operas given throughout the season at the Marie Theatre in St Petersburg and at the Opera House in Moscow. On two evenings a week, Wednesday and Sunday, it gives a special performance devoted entirely to the ballet. Moreover, some of the less distinguished dancers perform from time to time at the People's Palace in St Petersburg. The country, therefore, may be said to get good value for its money.

Attached to the great theatres, primarily reserved as homes of ballet, is the Imperial School of Dancing, which is of course supported by the State. The pupil—boy or girl—is entered at the age of about nine or ten. After the necessary nomination has been secured, a stringent examination with regard to health, intelligence, beauty of form and natural gracefulness has to be passed before the child is finally accepted. Mr Rothay Reynolds, who has an intimate knowledge of Russian life, gives an interesting account of the training:

"The school contains a great room for dancing, with a floor sloped at the same angle as that of the stage at the Marinsky Theatre. Here one may see a class of merry boys instructed in their art. A master, usually one of the best dancers in the theatre, shows them the steps and movements to be learnt, and half-a-dozen do their best to copy him. After ten minutes they go and rest, and a second batch comes forward. The boys seem to enjoy the work, and even when they are supposed to be resting some of them will continue to practise and give each other friendly hints. In another and similar room is the girls' class, where the method is the same. Then there is a room with many toilet-tables on which greasepaints are set out and with mirrors and electric lights arranged exactly as at the theatre. Here the pupils assemble for lessons in make-up. A boy has to learn to transform himself into a Chinese or an old man or a beautiful young Greek, and he has to pass examinations at different points of his school career in this art. I remember once meeting a young man in the waiting-room of a Polish dentist" (he goes on to relate). "He told me he had toothache and a nervous break-down, brought on he believed by the strain of a difficult examination. I asked what were the subjects of the examination. 'French,' he said, 'because we must be cultured, dancing, the history of dancing, and painting my face.' I had the curiosity to ask where this unusual curriculum was followed. 'At the Imperial School of Ballet,' he said, mentioned his name with the air of one who felt that he ought to have been recognised, and added: 'Thank heaven I've passed, and now I am a *premier danseur* . It is a delightful life, and when I am too old to dance the State will give me a pension.'"

THE RUSSIAN BALLET

AN UNDRESS REHEARSAL

The pupil at the Imperial Ballet School receives in fact a sound secondary education. Four hours a day are devoted to dancing during the eight years he is at school. While still at school the children occasionally appear on the stage in special *ballets d'enfants* . They also take part in "crowds" in operas where children are needed, as in the first act of Tchaikovsky's *Dame de Pique* . At seventeen they begin their career as members of the *corps de ballet* , from which the most proficient rise upwards, through the various grades of *coryphée* , *second sujet* , *premier sujet* , *première danseuse* or *ballerina* , and *ballerina assoluta* . The dancer retires, after eighteen years' service, at thirty-five—only artists of exceptional merit are permitted to continue after that age—and receives a pension of from one hundred and twenty pounds to two hundred and sixty pounds a year.

140

The fine quality of the performances of the Russian ballet is undoubtedly due in the first place to the prolonged and thorough training, not only of the principal dancers but of each individual performer. An average of five or six hours' dancing a day is the rule rather than the exception; for a ballet that is to be performed at night is always rehearsed during the day, however many times it may have been given before. The counsel of Carlo-Blasis, the eighteenth-century ballet-master is fulfilled to the letter: "Il faut encore étudier," he wrote, "lors même qu'on sera tout-à-fait formé.... Dans la musique, dans la peinture, etc., l'on n'a pas besoin d'un travail aussi opiniâtre pour conserver ce que l'on sait. L'art du danseur, comme tous ceux d'exercice, ne jouit pas de cet avantage." In the Russian ballet there is a perfect co-operation between the performers and an all-round technical excellence quite unlike anything that has ever been seen in this country.

Moreover the art of the male dancer, which had almost died out in other countries, has not only been kept alive in Russia but has been developed equally with that of the ballerina. The "principal boy" of the English stage is, as we know, always a girl. A note of character and energy disappeared from the ballet when it became solely the medium of feminine dancing. The strength and breadth of the Russian ballet have gained enormously by the retention and development of male dancing. Indeed its virility is one of the most striking features. The fierceness of the warrior dances in *Prince Igor* and the adroitness of the dance of buffoons in *Le Pavillon d'Armide* are among its most memorable achievements. *Scheherazade* without Nijinsky would be like *Hamlet* without the Prince of Denmark. We realise now that without the masculine element the ballet is as incomplete as an orchestra without the bass.

In Russia the music of the ballet has received the same careful consideration as the choregraphy. In some cases, music which was not written specially for the purpose has been adapted to the uses of the ballet. But latterly it has been the custom of the directors to apply to the leading composers of the day for ballet music written expressly for a given subject. In earlier times it was of course the custom for composers to write the music for the ballets that were interpolated in the opera. Tchaikovsky was one of the first to compose a ballet independent of opera and complete in itself. This was *The Sleeping Beauty* , first presented in 1890, in his own opinion the best thing he ever did, with the exception of his opera, *Eugène Onegin* . He showed his recognition of the necessity of an absolute co-ordination among the collaborators of the ballet by working in accordance with the suggestions of the choregrapher. The *maître de ballet* , after composing the design of the dances that were to express the spirit and action of the piece, sent to the musician a detailed schedule of the music required; thus:

No. 1. Musique douce, 64 mesures.

No. 2. L'arbre s'éclaire. Musique pétillant de 8 mesures.

No. 3. L'entrée des enfants. Musique bruyante et joyeuse de 24 mesures, etc.

Casse-Noisette , another ballet by the same composer, appeared in 1892. The original and powerful music of Borodin has been pressed into the service of the ballet, and entire ballets have been written by Rimsky-Korsakov, Glazounov and Arensky. In the execution of the music there is the same specialisation. The leaders of the orchestra qualify specially for the ballet, having no part in the orchestra at any other time.

It is clear, therefore, that in Russia the ballet has long been regarded as a serious art-form. A keen and intelligent criticism and an enthusiastic public interest provide it with that bracing atmosphere without which it is difficult for any composite form of art to thrive. On the nights devoted exclusively to the ballet, the large Marianski Theatre is so crowded that it is difficult to obtain a seat. Most of the stalls and boxes are subscribed for, and the people renew their subscriptions year after year. Mr Rothay Reynolds relates how, when an elderly gentlemen who for a great number of years had had a seat in the front row suddenly died, a friend of his rushed to the theatre and offered the young lady at the box-office twenty guineas if she would secure him the seat. "Alas!" she said, "I have already received over a hundred applications."

When the Russian ballet was being performed for the first time at Covent Garden, an enthusiast was heard to express his intention of emigrating to Russia in order to see the ballet in its true home. If he had carried out his intention it is to be feared that he would have suffered grievous disappointment. For it is a great misapprehension to suppose that the Russian ballet as it has been seen in Paris and London is typical of the official ballet at St Petersburg and Moscow. When the Diaghilew company first appeared at the Theatre du Châtelet, the republican convictions of Paris received a shock. Could any good thing come out of Tsardom? Had autocracy succeeded where the alliance of liberty, fraternity and equality had failed? Was it then true that venerable tradition, assisted by a bureaucratic regime, was a kinder nursing mother to the arts than the revolutionary spirit? Little by little the truth leaked out. The Russian ballet, which had been welcomed as the most modern manifestation of theatrical art, was not traditional but revolutionary. It was not the child of the official art of St Petersburg but the outcast. Its leaders were dangerous innovators whom the intransigent conservatives had expelled as hastily as if they had been political agitators. Paris was reassured.

The truth is that the excellence of the Imperial School of Ballet of which I have spoken is an excellence of method and technique rather than of spirit and conception. In ideals the Imperial Ballet has not travelled far from those of Milan in the earlier part of the nineteenth century.

It has elaborated and refined, but it has not greatly widened them. The visitor at the St Petersburg Opera House would discover that the unmeaning and unbeautiful acrobatics of an earlier day have not yet altogether disappeared. He would find that the ballet in *Aida* , for example, does not differ in many material points, excepting always the accomplishment of the performers, from what he has been accustomed to see in Milan or Vienna. It was in Russia that the spirit of criticism gave rise to new ideas, but the exponents of these new ideas came into sharp collision with the authorities at the Imperial theatres of St Petersburg and Moscow.

The spectacles which have been seen in London and Paris—some of which have never been produced in Russia—are the production of a group of daring and subversive artists, whom M. Serge de Diaghilew, the organiser of the ballets, has gathered round him—notably M. Fokine, the choregraphic director, MM. Leon Bakst and Benois, the designers of the scenery and costume, M. Tcherepnin, the musical composer and conductor, and of course M. Nijinsky and Mme Karsavina. M. Fokine, it is true, is the assistant ballet-master at the St Petersburg Opera, but he is said to be in command there only at the rarest intervals. M. Bakst has not worked for the Imperial theatres, and M. Tcherepnin comes, not from the St Petersburg Opera, but from the Conservatorium, where he is in charge of the orchestral class. They are able, of course, to avail themselves of the marvellous technical powers of the dancers who have joined them, practically all of whom were trained at the Imperial School of Ballet; but few of these are now regular members of the corps, and Nijinsky, the greatest genius of them all, recently received his formal discharge at the hands of the St Petersburg authorities. Long tradition, careful science and State patronage helped to make of the Imperial Ballet an elaborate, smoothly-working and faultless piece of theatrical mechanism; it only wanted the breath of genius to give it artistic life.

What then are the essential characteristics which differentiate the "revolutionary" Russian ballet from the traditional ballet as

Photograph: Gersche

it has hitherto been known both in Russia and elsewhere? The essential difference is to be found, not in technique, but in idea. The ballet has been brought into relation with life. Dancing, which had its origin in the most elemental emotions, gradually strayed further and further from its source, until in the ballet it lost its last remnant of vital significance. The ballet was relegated to a kind of barren limbo of the imagination; it was the *mise en scène* of the fairy tale; none of the echoes of the real world ever disturbed its enchanted silence; no excitement, no passion, no humour, was permitted to relax the fixity of its unmeaning smile. It was supposed to be structurally incapable of supporting anything more weighty than merely gossamer fancies, eternal variations upon the themes of coquetry —invitation and refusal, pursuit and evasion. Such inconsequential argument as there was served only to introduce a series of independent dances which were quite unrelated to any central inward idea. The ballet's complete sterility of idea was acquiesced in as a necessary condition of its existence. It was an artificial and somewhat withered paradise from which the river of life was carefully diverted. The work of the revolutionaries was to open the sluice-gates and let in the fertilising flood of vital emotion. The ineffectual rhythms of the dance were suddenly caught up into the masterful rhythms of life itself. What is revolutionary in the new ballet is the power to rouse and trouble the imagination. The innovators have extended the range of the ballet, a range as wide as that of the drama—one is tempted to say wider, for not only does it express a minute grace as choice as the grouping of the petals of a rose, but at times its huge leaping rhythms throb with an unconstrained and elemental violence, all too shattering for the formal mould of speech.

147

If the aim of the new movement is the strict subjection of the ballet to an artistic idea which shall express a high emotional impulse, the means by which it is attained is no less novel and characteristic. The ballet is a composite form of art, at once plastic, decorative and musical. Its success therefore depends upon an intimate collaboration between its composers, the choregraphic designer, the painter and the musician. An obviously necessary condition?—yes, but one which until the advent of the revolutionary ballet had been considerably neglected. Its neglect had resulted in the production of a mosaic of more or less artistic effects, jarring and warring among themselves. Too often the dance did not concur with the action. The steps were considered not as a means of expression, a language, but only as a brilliant exercise, without more signification than an acrobatic performance. Occasionally, as in the production of Tchaikovsky's *Sleeping Beauty* , the musician and the ballet-master worked in accord, but more often independently. The scene-painter produced a finished and usually photographic picture without any thought of the placing of the performers in the scene. The costumier, again, was accorded his own sweet will, and added his private inharmonious notes to the general discord. The new composers worked on the principle that there was not one design of the dance, another of the music and a third of the *décor*, but one design, one rhythm, one dominating impulse of the whole. In their ballets, the lines, the colours and the movements together interpret the spirit and the action, mutually reinforcing one another and producing a cumulative effect of strength and beauty, which at once grips and delights us.

If one of the collaborators of the revolutionary ballet has impressed upon it his personality more strongly than another it is M. Leon Bakst. He belongs to the new romantic school of painting, though he himself prefers to call it the new classical school, which is in full revolt against the illusion that the realists have set up as the final aim of art. He is a member of the Salon d'Automme, a pioneer and leader of the art movement which seeks to apply the principles of "post-Impressionism" to the decoration of the stage. The importance, not to say the pre-eminence, of the place which he claims in the theatre for the decorator, is best stated in his own words. "I believe," he says, "the time for the conventional producer to arrange the sunshine and shadow of the 'scene' has passed for ever. The peculiar form of 'mental' intelligence which has dominated the theatre for so many years is about to be replaced by the plastic intelligence, and the tone of the ensemble will be determined by the painter. The evolution of the

DANSE ORIENTALE

AFTER A DESIGN BY LÉON BAKST

theatre is towards a plastic ideal, and the action of a piece, sometimes full of invention, is weak and ineffective if it has not been conceived according to an artistic vision; just as an exaggerated 'literary' picture repels a true connoisseur. So give place to the painter in the theatre—and a leading place. It is the painter who should now (taking the place of the erudite director) create everything, know everything, foresee everything and organise everything. It is the painter who must be master of the situation, understand its finesse and decide the style of the piece. To his plastic judgment and taste must be subordinated the thousand details which compass the imposing ensemble of a fine work of the theatre."

How thoroughly M. Bakst's personality enters into the least details of the scene is evident in the two ballets which he has staged most brilliantly —*Cléopâtre* and *Scheherazade* . He introduces the "leitmotiv" into the scene and uses it as effectively as the musician. Rimsky-Korsakov's overture in *Scheherazade* does not more vividly suggest the sultry, sensual, Oriental atmosphere with its lurking brutalities than do the voluptuous lines and sinister colours of the artist. The feeling is continued in the costumes, which are not only fitly adjusted to the languorous movements of the dancers but also serve to carry out the colour-scheme of the scene. Each dress is a note of colour, chosen as carefully as an artist forms his tone upon the palette, and placed in its proper relation to the whole.

But the keynote of M. Bakst's art is simplicity and severity. "The painter of the future demands a severe style," he says, "because the excess of detail has become intolerable to him." Realism he abhors no less than pedantry of detail. He seeks to suggest the mood and not to photograph the event. His most gorgeous effects are obtained by an economy of material, which in comparison with one of the modern successful, over-propertied Shakespearian productions might seem positively parsimonious. And what he can achieve when he limits himself to the minimum of material may be seen in *Le Carnaval*, in which the two roguish sofas are probably the most eloquent and expressive properties ever placed upon the stage. Simplicity, suggestion, style—these are the qualities of M. Bakst's work in the theatre, and, above all, that all-embracing rhythm which, uniting with the rhythm of the music and the dance, helps to create one unity of colour, sound and movement.

Perhaps this is not the place to speak of the wide-reaching effect of the revolutionary ballet upon the general world of art. The colour and design of Leon Bakst's scenes, the provocative gestures of Nijinsky's dancing, the strange and startling patterns of the dancers, have suggested to artists a new source of inspiration, which in Paris at all events has already not been without its influence on their work. The ballet is in the van of the artistic movement of the day, and the dance, through the ballet, has attained a position which it has never held since the days of ancient Greece—being once more received into its proper and inseverable fellowship with music and the plastic arts.

CHAPTER X

THE REPERTORY OF THE RUSSIAN BAL-LET

T HE Russian ballets are based upon an endless variety of themes, but the dancing may be said to draw its inspiration from three sources. First and foremost, of course, is the traditional method of the old Italian masters. This is the mother tongue of the ballet, which is spoken from Copenhagen to Moscow, with only the least perceptible trace of local accent. But this common language the Russians have refined to a purity unknown elsewhere; from being the vehicle of the stiff rhetoric of the conventional ballet, they have transformed it into a flexible speech, in which they have been able to utter such gem-like poems as *Le Spectre de la Rose* , *Le Carnaval* and *Les Sylphides* . Next, they have gone for inspiration to their own national dances. They have refreshed the stage with the bracing air of the steppes. In the Polovtsian dances of *Prince Igor* they have given to an art that was nurtured in courts and has always moved with courtly grace, the tigerish motions of a full-blooded barbaric life. Finally they have enlarged the scope of the ballet by making use of the classical and Oriental dance. And for the sources of the classical dance they have gone not only to Greece but to Egypt. The theme of *Cléopâtre* is really the Egyptian attitude, just as the theme of *Scheherazade* is the Eastern attitude.

The Diaghilew ballet has an extensive repertory, wide enough to display to the full the genius of the composers and the talents of the dancers. Naturally, during the six seasons in which it has appeared in

Paris, its large variety has been better exhibited there than in London. The principal pieces which have been given at Covent Garden are *Le Pavillon d'Armide* , *Le Carnaval* , *Prince Igor* , *Les Sylphides* , *Le Spectre de la Rose* , *Cléopâtre* , *Scheherazade* .

Le Pavillon d'Armide is a link with the old conventional ballet. The fable is full of unreason. The pavilion is a spacious apartment in an old French château, deriving its name from the personage who forms the subject of a piece of Gobelin tapestry on the wall. To this castle comes one night a storm-belated traveller. He is hospitably entertained by the wicked marquis, the owner of the castle, who is an amateur magician of considerable attainments. After admiring the pictured figure of Armide, he falls asleep. As he sleeps the figures on the tapestry come to life, and he is transported in dream to the Court of Armide, where her captive knights dance in a chain of roses. He conceives a grand passion for the princess, and the king, whom he does not recognise to be the wizard marquis, blesses their union. The magic Court vanishes and the traveller wakes to find himself still in the bare, dawn-lit chamber. When the marquis enters to ask how he has slept he recognises with horror that he is none other than the king in the dream. And yet it was not wholly a dream, for at the same time he finds the actual golden scarf which Armide had given to him in plighting her troth. He knows himself to have been the victim of a fatal enchantment, and thereupon somewhat irrelevantly dies.

M. Fokine has made of this irrational fable the framework of a number of dances which display the perfect unity and discipline of the dancers. But Nijinsky, as the servant of the traveller, and Karsavina, as Armide, are scarcely given adequate scope for their originality and faculty of interpretation. The thing is good of its kind—it is the perfection of the traditional *ballet d'action* —but it has been done before. The most satisfying feature of the performance is a dance of seven buffoons, of whom the premier buffoon is M. Rosai. Incidentally they execute several steps which technically are among the most difficult in the dancer's repertory. But the chief merit of their display is its grotesque wit, the mimicry of the half-human antics of marionettes, executed with a faultless rhythmical precision.

The decoration was devised by M. Benois and, at all events

WASLAW NIJINSKY

as it was presented at Covent Garden, it cannot be said to have been really successful. The pavilion had no other hint of a fatal spell than that which the lowered lights could suggest; the Court of Armide, who was surely twin-sister to "La Belle Dame sans Merci," might have been made to evoke some vision akin to that which Keats saw of "pale kings and princes too, pale warriors, death-pale were they all." But, perhaps largely owing to the faulty lighting, it was a rather garish spectacle, a noisy conflict of pure reds, greens and blues. Only for a moment did the scene really live,—when the mists began to wash round the battlements, the colours fused together in a trembling twilight, the tumult of the action died away and the motionless figures gazed after the victim traveller led away by his fatal lover.

But doubtless the composers of the ballet do not claim for it any special seriousness of intention. We are to take it or leave it as a simple *ballet d'action* of the conventional school, no more than a groundwork for some very brilliant and elaborate dancing. It is only a failure when judged by canons which we should not think of applying to any ballet but that of M. Diaghilew.

The theme of *Le Carnaval* may be regarded as even more flippant, but it expresses a series of purely musical ideas, and moreover it shows how the ballet can be made as witty as dialogue. It is an adaptation by M. Fokine of Schumann's well-known pianoforte solo. Hardly a note has been added to Schumann's music or taken away from it by the four composers who have skilfully provided the instrumentation—Rimsky-Korsakov, Liadov, Glazounov and Tcherepnin. Not only has Schumann's work lost nothing of its original savour, but rather it has gained in expression and brilliance. In this fantasy, beloved of pianists, Schumann sought to represent various personages whom the ballet presents to us in material form. The composer's explanation of the work was given to Moscheles, to whom he wrote: "The *Carnaval* was written mostly for different occasions, and, excepting three or four of the pieces, is all founded on the notes A. S. (A flat), C. H (B natural), which form the name of a little town in Bohemia where I had a musical friend, and which, curiously enough, are also the only musical letters in my name. I wrote the titles later.... As a whole, the work has absolutely no artistic merit; but individually the various states of feeling seem to me interesting." The pieces are written round a number of imagined characters—Arlequin, Columbine, Estrella, Chiarina, Pierrot, Pantalon, Papillon, Florestan, Eusebius. The Chiarina was supposed to be Madame Schumann, the Estrella, as Schumann told Moscheles, "a name such as one writes under portraits to impress the picture on the mind," and in Florestan and Eusebius he represented himself.

M. Fokine has been wiser than to impose upon these irresponsible creatures of the musician's fancy the burden of a formal plot. They merely flit across the stage in a succession of amorous episodes which take place during a masked fête—Pierrot deceived and suffering, Pantalon duped, Eusebius romantic, Florestan impetuous, Chiarina sentimental and Estrella turbulent.

M. Bakst, the decorator, has completed the ballet by making it an exquisitely delicate artistic whole. The tinsel glitter and vast expenditure of means upon which the conventional ballet is usually built up has been utterly discarded. In its place is a simplicity verging on bareness, an economy of material in which every tone and line has an individual value, and bespeaks the guidance of a single directing mind. The curtain rises upon an almost empty scene, the ante-chamber of a ball-room. The backcloth is a broad band of purplish blue uplifting a deep frieze of red tulips. The furniture of the scene consists solely of two droll tiny striped sofas, crouching against the black and gold dado, which instantly put us on the tiptoe of expectation and give the keynote of airy mockery that characterises the piece. Suddenly the tall curtains of this fastidious ante-chamber are parted and Chiarina and Estrella, followed by their distraught lovers, scamper in and out again. Gradually the room fills with crinolined figures, flashing amorous glances through the slits of their silk masks, and comical gentlemen whose quaintly cut green and golden brown jackets seem to travesty their woeful passions. The gaiety of the music dances through the shifting lights and softly flowing lines. And through this happy and heartless crowd moves the tragic

LEONTIEV AND LEPOUKHAVA

IN *Le Carnaval*

Photograph: Bert, Paris

figure of Pierrot, whose unrequited love his fellows make a mock of. His costume and attitude are a masterpiece of design. His sleeves, a world too long, droop far below his finger-tips, forming a scheme of painful angles which most poignantly express his grotesque and lamentable passion.

Of course this foolish, fluttering world of philanderers we never for an instant really believe in. They are the graceful, graceless figures of a Conder fan come to life. They are as hollow as the porcelain amorists our grandmothers were wont to put upon their chimney-pieces. We laugh at their impatient ardours as well as at their harrowing griefs. Even Pierrot we refuse to take seriously. He himself does not expect it—else he would not pretend that Chiarina were a butterfly and attempt to catch her beneath his conical white hat, and then, lifting it cautiously half-an-inch from the ground, make a gesture of farcical despair at finding her escaped. The whole ballet has the effect of transporting us into an unreal world—not a fantastic and fairy world, but a half-familiar world, a Lilliputian world, in which all the serious traffic of our hearts is mocked and parodied. We laugh because we do not recognise the likeness of these parabolic puppets to ourselves, for if we did we should surely weep. If its intention were a shade more serious the ballet would become a sermon, with *Vanitas vanitatum* for its text; it carefully stops short, however, at that indefinite border-line where trifling passes into satire, but not before it has shown us that the ballet can be made the vehicle of ironic laughter.

If *Le Carnaval* is gently satiric, *Prince Igor* , in its suggestion of historic catastrophe, is epic. The *Danses Polovtsiennes* , of which the ballet chiefly consists, are taken from an opera by Borodin—"a rather tedious opera," it has been called—founded upon a Russian ballad of doubtful authenticity. It is a case in which the dance is not merely an interlude in the opera, but the very life and soul of it. The story is of no interest; it is effaced by the terrible intensity of the barbaric dancing. The scene takes us to the

Russian steppes. The design is by Roehrich—a Tartar camp standing out against a landscape that is sinister with a wrathful, blood- dark glow. "How excellently every means that the theatre offers has been made use of to produce the desired effect!" writes a discriminating critic in an admirable analysis of the qualities that make so resistless an appeal to the imagination; "the menace of the coming cloud of barbarians that is to lie for centuries on the desolate face of Russia—not the loud blustering of a Tamburlaine the Great, but the awful quiet vigour, half melancholy, half playful, of a tribe that is itself but a little unit in the swarm; the infinite horizons of the steppe, with the line of the burial tumuli stretching away to endless times and places, down the centuries, into Siberia; the long-drawn, resigned, ego-less music (Borodin drew his themes from real Tartar-Mongol sources); the women that crouch unconscious of themselves, or rise and stretch lazy limbs, and in the end fling themselves carelessly prone when their dance is over; the savage-joyful panther-leaping of the men; the stamping feet and quick nerve-racking beat of the drum; and, more threatening than all, the gambolling of the boys, like kittens unwittingly preparing themselves for the future chase."

The scene is a symbol of that peril of the barbarians which has always lain on the remote frontiers of civilisations. The tremendous rhythm with which the warriors come bounding down the stage communicates a sense of exhilaration not altogether unmixed with terror. The dance quickens to the frenzy of delirium. Its triumphant motions seem to throb with all those volcanic forces which one knows to be slumbering always in the heart of man: all the eternal unrest of his blood, all his sheer delight in life and strife, all that central fire which kindles from age to age the conflagrations of war and revolution. It is probably the most exciting presentment of barbaric frenzy the stage has ever seen. Considered as an artistic achievement it is astounding. For it must be remembered that this effect

of surging tumult is only obtained by the most rigid discipline, by unanimity and a perfectly calculated precision of rhythm.

From epic the composers of the ballet turn to lyricism in *Le Spectre de
la Rose* . The music is Weber's "Invitation à la Valse" as scored by Berlioz;
the pantomimic text is suggested by a poem

KARSAVINA AND NIJINSKY

of Théophile Gautier. It is the story of a young girl who falls asleep in her chair, worn out with the fatigue and excitement of the ball. In her dream the rose which she holds in her hand becomes a genie, who dances with her, kisses her and disappears at break of day.

Here again Leon Bakst has created a scene of grave yet tender simplicity, with the fine, strict lines of a Beardsley drawing. The girl's bedroom is a scheme of white and blue; on one side an alcove with a bed, on the other a plain white dressing-table. The windows open upon a garden. Moonlight falls upon the floor. It is all very intimate, reposeful and virginal. The girl wears a simple white frock, the spirit of the rose a fantastic costume of crimson and purple petals.

The *pas de deux* is executed by Nijinsky and Karsavina. Nothing could be more graciously conceived than Mme Karsavina's representation of the girl dancing in her dream. With half-closed eyes she rises slowly from her chair and sways across the room in a kind of swoon, following the gentle guidance of the flower-spirit. Then as her dream becomes more vivid she recovers a little strength and dances of her own motion, but always with a suggestion of unconsciousness, as though less to the music of the orchestra than to some dimly remembered melody of the brain. As in the manner of episodes in a dream, she darts into swift movements, which pass again into languor. For an instant the kiss awakens her, she looks round upon the familiar aspect of her room, then the tired head sinks again upon her breast. It is a very gentle rendering of the mood of recollection and happy, unperturbed trance.

In this dream-ballet Nijinsky is a being of amazing agility and grace. He is as light upon the air as a rose petal. He contrives to bring into his dancing something of the gentleness of the moonlit night and the fragrance of the dawn. He shows himself as capable of delicate and almost womanly motion as he is of masculine vivacity and vigour. And when he floats out through the open window back to his rose-garden, he almost persuades one for the moment that he has discovered the secret of human flight.

In *Les Sylphides* the producers have been daring enough to forget to be modern. They have rehabilitated a form of ballet for which a few years ago one would have said there could be no resurrection. The piece has no action, no colour, no idea, almost no sentiment—it is choregraphy pure and simple, as abstract as mathematics. It is described vaguely as a romantic reverie. The romantic note is sounded by the dim backcloth of ruins and moonlight by M. Benois. The score of dancers wear the traditional costume, pure white, the skirt rather long, as Taglioni might have worn it.

The piece, however, has no connection with the ballet of a similar name in which Taglioni made her great success. It is an adaptation of various compositions of Chopin, which have been orchestrated by Glazounov and other composers. The orchestral version is less faithful to the original than that of Schumann's *Carnaval*, but the additions are all in the spirit of the whole. Nijinsky and Karsavina each danced a mazurka, and together in the Valse in C sharp minor they executed a *pas de deux* that was a perfectly finished artistic achievement. For the finale there was the Valse brillante in E flat, in which the grouping of the dancers displayed the skill of M. Fokine at its highest.

Les Sylphides is somewhat in the nature of a challenge, and it must be admitted that it is a successful challenge. In it the producers claim that the purely musical and choregraphic interests are sufficient. Of its kind it is no less than perfect. It is from beginning to end a rhythmic flow of flawless gestures, which make a rounded whole of a chaste and immaculate quality like that of the finest sculpture. More remarkable than the steps is the purity of the lines of the arms, interweaving like the overarching branches of a forest glade or the groining of the aisle of a Gothic cathedral. Yet was there not perhaps a moment when the disconcerting thought intruded itself: Supposing the ballet were always to move in this atmosphere of perfect calm? Without a doubt *Les Sylphides* gained some of its charm from its place in sequence of the ballets. As an interlude among pieces of more violent action, it had the repose of a statue in the midst of canvases hot with colour and tumultuous with movement.

LES SYLPHIDES
Photograph: Bert, Paris.

If it is in such pieces as *Les Sylphides* , *Le Carnaval* and *Le Spectre de la Rose* that the composers of the ballets with their coadjutant mimes most deftly lay the privy net for beauty, they ensnare her, more brutally perhaps, but none the less surely in the Oriental pageants with their closely knit web of line and tone and rhythm. For these many-faceted compositions, ballet is perhaps an incomplete expression, and we should substitute the term, "mimodrama." Dancing plays a more subordinate part in them than in the ballet proper. It falls into a natural relation to the ensemble, and yet the dance, in the exotic world here represented to us, is the apt, indeed the only conceivable gesture.

Cléopâtre is a name of ominous import and prepares us for voluptuous and sombre passion. We are transported to a temple on the banks of the Nile. This scene is the supreme achievement of M. Bakst's art. It represents an immense stone forecourt which might be none other than the great Hall of Columns built by the father of Rameses the Great. But the artist is contemptuous of pedantic archæological detail—he seeks only to impress, one might rather say to stun, the senses by a vision of grandiose and sinister masonry. This effect is obtained by simple lines and vast proportions. The towering walls, the procession of squat, colossal columns, the gigantic intimidating statues on either flank, fill the scene with a sense of awe and a premonition of disaster. It is noteworthy that M. Bakst himself has said that the painters of the future will take for their subjects man and stone. In this scene he has given to the dumb and eternal stone a voice of tragedy. He has made of these sexless caryatides a kind of chorus, the immortal and ironic spectators of the comedy of human life.

Broken by the compacted row of columns, we see the flowing waters of the Nile, violet and emerald—fit stream to bear the burnished barge of Cleopatra with its poop of beaten gold and perfumed purple sails. Perhaps it is this visiting river that gives the note of expectancy which is so often present in M. Bakst's scenes. Satisfying the scene is in itself, but the eternal stone awaits its fugitive inhabitant—man. With all reverence, preceded by maidens strewing rose-leaves, the negro slaves bear in the regal litter. Egypt's queen is lifted as carefully as a jewel out of its casket and stands immobile as an image while her servants divest her of her silken wrappings. Then, with an attitude of languor unutterable, weary with the deceitful satiety of her desires, supported by her abject crouching slaves, she passes to her couch.

The part of Cleopatra was played in Paris by Ida Rubinstein, at Covent Garden by Seraphima Astafieva. The rôle is one not for a dancer, but for a mime, pure and simple. These artists in their studied and astonishing gestures appear to have created a new art of pantomime. Ida Rubinstein—and perhaps the same may be said of Astafieva—has trained the body to a silent speech outvying in subtlety the subtlest of spoken words. The least of her gestures takes an importance so grave and so surprising that it becomes henceforth impossible to dissociate it from the personage whom she evokes. Her hieratic attitudes, with their meticulous and adorable gaucherie, their touching faults of perspective, derive from the Egyptian bas-relief and the Italian primitives. The unexpected lines of the slowly moving limbs are instinct with the very genius of *plastique* .

Little wonder that the noble Amoun leaves his love, to whom he has plighted his troth but a moment before, and is drawn by the fatal magnetism of this odalisque of a woman. At his audacity the listless queen leaps into a momentary tigerish passion; and then, moved by the young man's beauty and willing to amuse her tedium with a new excitement, she promises him the fulfilment of his dreams at the price of his life. As the infatuated youth fondles her upon her couch, the court fills with the retinue of slaves and begins to throb with the luminous coils of their dance.

The lines of the dance repeat the all-embracing lines of the architecture. The attitudes of the dancers are freely modelled upon the poses of the figures depicted on the ancient Egyptian monuments. When M. Bakst sets his figures in motion, he is mindful of their relation to the *décor* . They are not set against the scene as against a background, but become actually a part of it. He constructs his picture so that the actors shall be the complement of the design and of the colour-scheme. His method has been thus

SERAPHIMA ASTAFIEVA

AS *Cleopatra*

Photograph: Dover Street Studios, Ltd.

described: "He places a number of pure, fresh colours on the stage. The colours are first placed in order of their relationship to each other, and thereafter arranged according to a complete gradation of tints. Thus he selects, say, six colours—red, orange, yellow, green, blue, violet. From these he evolves six rows of colours, starting with each colour at full pitch, and gradating it till he reaches the lowest, subtlest, and most Whistler-like key. Then he sets all these reds and yellows and blues and greens revolving. The effect is indescribable. The whole scene begins to pulsate. The walls and the floor clothe themselves with designs of perfectly designed rhythmical lines. Masses move in all directions according to a law of ordered disorder. The air becomes dense with a quivering sheen of colour so violently contrasted, yet so harmonious."

But the distinguishing characteristic of *Cléopâtre* is the subordination of the dancing to the *décor*. In spite of the intensity of the frenzy of madly whirling limbs, the spectator is never allowed to forget the grim stone witnesses of the human tumult. With something malevolent in the gaze of their obliquely set eyes, the erect, abiding figures glance down upon the momentary riot. The men of stone are mightier than the men of flesh. Suddenly, when passion is storming through the veins, we are reminded of the triviality and transience of everything human. Here again is that ironic note which in so many of the Russian ballets forms a menacing undertone to their music.

A hush falls upon the dancers. The night of love is over and Cleopatra is about to take toll of her lover. With an incredibly cruel gesture she passes, or rather insinuates, the cup brimmed with poisons. The youth drinks. Cleopatra, with greedy, curious eyes, watches him stagger and writhe in his death-agony. Then this newest sensation of excitement fails her, her unutterable languor repossesses her, and, leaning upon her bending slaves, she passes slowly beneath the towering portal, along the terrace by the river, and her retinue dumbly follow her.

Then the artist speaks his last unerring word. The priest covers the prostrate body with a black pall. The voided forecourt resumes its immensity of space. A warm flush clothes the broad surfaces of the columns; brightness lies on the river; and the single stain of black sets the seal of tragedy upon the empty scene.

Scheherazade is an illuminated page torn from the book of "The Thousand and One Nights." The music, the scenery, the dances, the costumes, the appointments, all the circumstances of the ballet are designed to create a heavy perfumed atmosphere of Eastern voluptuousness. The severity and simplicity of the Egyptian temple is exchanged for the semi-barbaric sumptuousness of the harem of an Arabian palace. A massive curtained canopy of an impure green stained with purple hangs in billowy folds over the scene; massy silvern lamps depend from a ceiling splendid with arabesques and floral designs; a latticed window gives upon a garden of tainted verdure; the floor is inlaid with blood-coloured porphyry. The sensuous lines of M. Bakst's *décor* are echoed in the throbbing waves of Rimsky-Korsakov's music. Here again is the complete sympathy between musician and decorator, which fuses these ballets into an organic whole. In spite of the wealth of the accessories, there is not an irrelevant line or tone; there is economy and constraint even in the splendour, so that the spectator receives an impression of singleness and unity like that of Greek drama.

At the very commencement the keynote is given in the dance of three odalisques, in which languor intertwines with the energy of desire. As the ballet proceeds the gust of passion blows more strongly, and the riot begins after the departure of the two sultans, when the Grand Eunuch unlocks first a bronze door, through which enter negroes clothed in copper-coloured costumes, and then a silver door, which gives entry to another band of negroes attired in silver. Zobeide, the favourite faithless wife of the sultan Schahriar, still remains without her consort. She crouches half fearfully against a curtain, which at last is pulled aside and her lover, a gorgeous negro in a golden dress, leaps upon her with one tremendous panther-like bound. Undoubtedly the climax of the ballet is reached in the ecstatic dances of Nijinsky as the slate-coloured negro. He has learnt a whole new grammar of grotesque, savage gestures. Part monkey, part tiger, part human, he fawns, he caresses, he grimaces, he passes from delirium to devotion, from awe to lust, his body elemental fire, motion, passion. At times his swiftness renders him momentarily almost invisible; at times he becomes a living boomerang, and after a marvellous circuit in space returns unerringly to his point of departure; one moment he is an arrow shot through the air, the next a crouching, servile beast worshipping the feet of his mistress. And in the mad final orgy he is the vortex of the swirling throng, the happy, leaping heart which shoots its ecstasy to the outermost limits of the coiling maze of lovers.

With a sound of dismay the music signals the return of the betrayed sultans. The harem becomes a slaughter-house. A flashing scimitar cuts down the golden negro. Zobeide drives the dagger into her breast and falls grasping the feet of her outraged lord.

A discerning critic has pointed out that perhaps the terrifying suggestiveness of *Scheherazade* lies not so much in the catastrophe of the plot as in the dreadful significance of Rimsky-Korsakov's music. "Passages that may have meant no more, as pure music, than the secrecy of the East and the plaintive mysteriousness of women (like that often-repeated passage on the first violin) get a new colour of tragic passion, of yearning in the shadow of death, from their allotment in the dramatic scheme. There is the sound of fate and murder, mingled with the saddest ironical comedy, in the insistent blast of the hunting horns. The swift huddling of deceitful wives, the tripping and scurrying, the wheedling of the old eunuch, the ravenous mien of the negroes, the magnificent stride and gesture of the fruit-bearing attendants, the complicated frenzy of the dance, the drama of fear and despair in Karsavina's proud rendering, leave a solemn impression beyond anything in those other fantastic ballets. How much depends upon the music it is hard to gauge—much more than one is disposed to admit at first; for the mind pouring stagewards through the eyes, receives the musical impressions half unconsciously, as a direct emotional influence, scarcely registered in the sensuous ear."

Of the other ballets which complete the repertory of the Diaghilew company, and which have not yet been seen in London —of *Petrouchka* , a Russian burlesque taken from an old folk-story, Harlequin in love with the clown's wife; of *Sadko* , a strange submarine drama; of *Narcisse* , an idyll which seeks to recapture the sylvan mood of ancient Greece—I will not attempt to give any description. Enough has been said to show that the revolutionary composers, with the co-operation of Nijinsky, Karsavina and a *corps de ballet* , every member of which is a tried artist, have given a new significance to the ballet, have indeed given a new art-form to the stage.

CHAPTER XI

THE RUSSIAN DANCERS

C OULD the Diaghilew ballet exist without Waslaw Nijinsky—this marvellous youth who is already a supreme master of the technique of dancing, who cannot make a gesture that has not a graceful or a witty significance, who has confounded Newton and demonstrated that the law of gravity is a figment of the scientists?

Nijinsky has danced ever since he was an infant. Both his mother and father were in the ballet at the Imperial theatre in Warsaw, where he sometimes danced with them. His first appearance was as a little Chinese with a pigtail, when he was yet only six years old. The serious study of his art began in 1898, when he entered the Imperial Ballet School at St Petersburg. He passed his final examinations in 1907, and danced at the Imperial theatres for a year and a half before he visited other countries. In 1909 he danced in the Russian Ballet at the Théâtre du Châtelet at Paris, and in the following year at the Opera. Subsequently he has appeared with the Diaghilew company in Berlin, Brussels, Rome, Monte Carlo and London. At Paris he caught typhoid, and when he was convalescent went to Venice, where he danced with Isadora Duncan. It is the place he loves best of all. Already, at the age of only twenty-one, he has received the enthusiastic applause of the most brilliant and exacting audiences of Europe; critics have minutely discussed and lavishly eulogised his dancing; artists have studied and reproduced his gestures; he has been the darling of society in half-a-dozen capitals—and yet the miracle is that he is untouched by conceit. He remains a modest, ingenuous youth, tireless in application, teachable, seeking continually to bring his art to a more precise perfection.

In February 1911 the world of the theatre was astounded to hear that Nijinsky had been asked to withdraw from the Imperial Opera at St Petersburg. Various ungrounded stories have been afloat as to the cause of the rupture, but the truth is that it was merely an incident, perhaps an inevitable one, in the antagonism between the traditional and revolutionary schools of the ballet. For a moment the older school triumphed, and Nijinsky left Russia to undertake the enterprise of the conquest of Europe.

The pretext which the officials seized upon to rid themselves of the young revolutionary was a detail of costume. Madame Kschesinskaya, the fixed star in the Imperial firmament, wished Nijinsky to appear with her in one of the ballets of the stereotyped Italian school. He, on the other hand, preferred to take the part of Loys in *Giselle* , the ballet by Gautier and d'Adam in which Grisi won her greatest triumph. He carried the day, and the ballet was produced at considerable expense. His costume, a *maillot* of yellow silk, was designed by Benois. He had some doubts as to whether it would be acceptable to the authorities, and therefore obtained special permission from the "commandant general" of the Imperial ballets to wear it. At the last moment one of the directors objected to the costume, and ordered Nijinsky to change it. The dancer expostulated, and as there was not sufficient time to replace it with another, the director did not insist. The evening on which he appeared for the first and last time in *Giselle* at the St Petersburg Opera, the Imperial box was full. The dancer was received by the whole house with the greatest enthusiasm. The Dowager Empress and the Grand Dukes were warm in their applause, and at the conclusion of the performance the Empress told one of the directors that she had never seen its equal. The next day, however, on the pretext that the *maillot* was objectionable, Nijinsky received notice that his services were no longer required. The repentance of the management came speedily, but the dancer declined their request that he should return. What influenced him probably not a little in his determination to leave was the fact that,

179

WASLAW NIJINSKY

for a dancer with his zest for work, his post at the Imperial Opera was more or less of a sinecure. The ballet, which only performed about six times a month, was too intermittent to give a proper scope for his activity.

With a dead complexion, lank, dun-coloured hair, high cheekbones, long and somewhat obliquely set eyes, Nijinsky has the racial characteristics of the Slav. His expression is one of a serenity that is untroubled by the glory of the present or the cares of the future. His eye is bright and expressive. In repose his face has a certain dreamy preoccupation, which at a word spoken or a sight that arrests his attention, passes swiftly into an absorbing interest in the life of the moment. His is clearly a highly-strung temperament—indeed he told me that what he found most difficult in his art was the conquest of the nerves.

Nijinsky has the genius for taking pains. A movement, a gesture, which upon the stage has often the appearance of a happy improvisation, is invariably the result of careful study. How searching is his preparation I only realised when I saw him one morning practising with Madame Karsavina on the stage at Covent Garden. His instructor, M. Cecchetti, a distinguished member of the Diaghilew company (he is the wicked marquis in *Le Pavillon d'Armide* , the Grand Eunuch in *Scheherazade*), took him through even the most elementary exercises with the severity of a drill sergeant. For the young dancer, however, it was not a mechanical routine, but a kind of play, into which he entered with a certain smiling gaiety. If he found that he was executing a movement imperfectly, he stopped short in the middle of it with a gesture of half-amused vexation and repeated it over and over again until he had made it faultless. The actual mastery of the technique appeared to him to be in itself a delight, and not, as with many dancers, a painful task-work. In his practice I found that the turns of his pirouettes and the cuts of his entrechats were more numerous than in the actual performance, for he never perverts the intention of the dance by introducing into it acrobatic feats merely for the sake of dazzling the spectator.

It is not altogether easy to analyse the qualities of Nijinsk y's dancing in virtue of which he is rightly regarded as the finest *danseur* of the age. Perhaps his chief merit consists in that very versatility which seems to conceal the pre-eminence of any single feature. He never repeats himself. His personality appears to inhabit not one but several bodies, or rather his personality itself is multiple. Did not one know that it were the fact, would it be possible to believe that the lustful negro of *Scheherazade* was one with the tender flower-spirit of *Le Spectre de la Rose* , or the impish and irresponsible Arlequin of *Le Carnaval* the same as the courteous and adoring page of *Le Pavillon d'Armide* ? He identifies himself in each ballet with the spirit of the action and of the music.

Nijinsky makes us understand that a gesture is, as Blake said of a tear, an intellectual thing. His gestures, by which I do not mean the technical steps, are different in manner and in spirit from those of the traditional Italian school. With the conventional gestures of the academies, which mimic such attitudes as men are supposed naturally to adopt when they perform certain actions or experience certain emotions, he will have nothing to do. Nijinsky's gestures mimic nothing. They are not the result of a double translation of idea into words, and words into dumb show. They are the mood itself. His limbs possess a faculty of speech. Wit is expressed in his Arlequin dance as lucidly as in an epigram. In *Le Spectre de la Rose* he dances a sonnet of delighted devotion. He makes credible the suggestion, intended satirically, that La Rochefoucauld's "Maximes" should be rendered choregraphically. His genius consists in a singular pliancy of the body to the spirit.

His technique is characterised by extreme brilliance and agility. He is weirdly grotesque or daintily graceful at will. Where he is perhaps lacking is in gravity and statuesque pose. Nijinsky does not realise the Pheidian ideal as perfectly as Mordkin, and therefore he can never be his equal in creating that impression of the glorious virility of a Greek statue, in whose firm lines a mighty strength lies sleeping. Nor have I ever seen him adequately represent the fierceness of human passion. Even in his *Scheherazade* dances there is not so much a deep exultation as a kind of schoolboy merriment. But these are the necessary limitations of a youthful body and

TAMAR KARSAVINA

a youthful spirit. Nor would we have it otherwise. We will leave the rest to time. The years will deepen and dignify his art. If he is too happy to enter into certain phases of the spirit we will gladly bear with his short-comings. We are content to take him as he is—the genial, leaping, happy dionysiac fawn!

It is interesting to record here some of his impressions and his remarks about himself.

"I love dancing to the music of Chopin," he says, "you see we are fellow-countrymen. I am not a Russian really; my parents were Poles, and I am a Catholic and not Orthodox. I always imagine that it is only a Pole who can really interpret Chopin; we understand the melancholy of his music."

With regard to the *milieu* of his performance he has said: "One thing I am determined not to do, and that is to go on the music-hall stage. I have had several tempting offers; but after all what is money? I think more of art than of money, and I refuse to be sandwiched between performing dogs and acrobats."

Before he appeared at Covent Garden he said, "I am frightened of London. I like the town, it is so big and serious, but the thought of dancing at Covent Garden makes me feel nervous."

After he had danced there, however, he was not nervous of criticising the Covent Garden audience. "They are not very demonstrative compared with the Parisians, but they are faithful, they seem to come again and again in great numbers. But they have a horrible habit—during the last piece on the programme there is always a constant stream of people going out. I think this is disgracefully ill-mannered, and I refuse now to dance in the last piece on the programme. I refuse to dance to an audience that is melting away—it is an insult to art. At Paris, all the times I have danced there, not a single person has stirred at a single performance until the curtain fell at the end. And here at London we end quite early—at eleven o'clock. That gives people plenty of time to get their suppers, doesn't it? Fortunately the stage at Covent Garden is conveniently big. It has one disadvantage—it does not slope at all. It is quite flat, so that when I was dancing there at first I kept falling forwards. "

Madame Karsavina, the *première danseuse* of the Diaghilew company, is in every way a fit colleague for the incomparable Nijinsky. Although still quite young, she is fast making for herself a reputation that will probably be second to none in the Russian ballet. Last year the retirement of Mademoiselle Preobrajenskaya from regular work and the withdrawal of Madame Pavlova left her an arduous task to fulfil in St Petersburg. In order to fill the gaps that she alone was capable of filling, she was obliged to study new parts which the retired dancers had made peculiarly their own—an undertaking of considerable delicacy. But her genius enabled her to draw even from the most exacting critics that quiet smile of inward appreciation which she has acutely declared to be the highest tribute to the artist. She is hard-working, very ambitious, and takes her art very seriously in all its branches.

Of her performances at Covent Garden, all were marked by such rare technique and instructed grace that it is difficult to put any one before another; but certainly she never surpassed her achievement in *Le Spectre de la Rose* . Her dancing caught the very spirit of a maiden's reverie, and nothing could have been more finely imagined than those transitions from languor into quick rushes of darting movement, which illustrate the abrupt and irrational episodes of a troubled dream. She was the very embodiment of faint desire. We felt, as it were, a breath of perfume, and were troubled in spite of ourselves. Moreover, the long partnership between the two performers seemed to have resulted in a very special and intimate harmony. For the most part they simply floated about the stage as though borne upon a common current of emotion. There was a marriage, not only between their bodily movements, but between their spirits, such as I have never noted in the union of any other dancers. In *Scheherazade* Madame Karsavina proved herself to be the possessor of a dramatic sense which the other ballets had not sufficiently displayed. As the faithless Zobeide, she mimed with astonishing subtlety an inward conflict of warring emotions, fear mingling with desire, rapture giving place to despair. Her gestures were charged with the same passionate significance as those of Ida Rubinstein and Astafieva.

ANNA PAVLOVA

Both her miming and her dancing were characterised by a certain natural softness of movement, the quality of languor rather than of passion, which was nevertheless consistent with the greatest firmness of outline.

While in Paris, Madame Karsavina sketched a comparison of the French and Russian ballets, which indicates her own conception of the art: "Our school is the same. We derive equal inspiration from the great traditions of the dance, bequeathed by Auguste Vestris and Jean-Georges Noverre. Only the French ballet has rested in these traditions, without troubling to renew them. The academic style of the French dancers is the same as that of a century ago. After having carefully studied these traditions and profited by them, we have sought something more. We have wished to present faithful images of the life round about us. Our epoch is finer, depend upon it, than any other. Human emotions have been refined or transformed. The spectacles of former times no longer move us very deeply. I have been to see *Coppelia* at the Opera. It is good, very good. But *Coppelia* is quite démodé. Really it is possible to imagine choregraphic arrangements more modern, more closely in touch with life—this fine and various and over-brimming life of to-day."

When Madame Anna Pavlova was leaving Russia, she parted with an old general, who was saying good-bye to her, with the farewell wish, "May all that is best be yours!" To this he replied, "How can the best be ours when you are depriving us of the very best we had?" Not every member of the Imperial ballet has yet visited Paris and London, and therefore it is difficult for those who have never been to Russia to speak in terms of comparison, but we are willing to believe in the justice of the general's appraisement.

Madame Pavlova received her training at the Imperial Ballet School at St Petersburg. She speedily passed upwards through the various ranks of the ballet, until she became *prima ballerina* at the Marianski Theatre. She made her début on the foreign stage at Munich, and subsequently appeared in Berlin, Vienna, Paris, and New York. When she came to London in 1910 she immediately had the town at her feet. London was at a disadvantage, however, compared with New York, for whereas in America she performed in the ballet, at the Palace Theatre in London she appeared exclusively in solo dances, or with her partner, Mikail Mordkin. The British amateur of the dance, therefore, has seen but a part of her genius, for that pure mimesis, in which she excels no less than in the actual dancing itself, requires for its full scope the interaction of characters which belongs to the ballet proper. She herself told me that she preferred playing in the ballet to dancing alone, but it is difficult to believe that her personality could find fuller expression than in the single dances in which she has the whole stage to herself. Moreover, when in England she was deprived of the splendid setting of the Russian *décor*, the backcloth at the Palace Theatre being a rather distracting and futile example of the British scene-painter's art.

Anna Pavlova is not merely a great executive, but a creative artist. She is more than a dancer, she is a lyric poet. One feels that she might equally well have chosen any other of the media of art for the expression of her emotion, but she has chosen her body—or perhaps rather her body has chosen her. This beautiful instrument she has refined to the most delicate sensibility and instructed in a perfect precision. As a piece of mechanism —if indeed mechanism be not too harsh a term for what in grace is wholly flower-like—it has been rendered as supple, just and exquisitely responsive as infinite pains could make it. It is perfectly equipped with swiftness, strength, delicacy. Only in the very greatest dancers does the body become the utter slave of the spirit, serving it with a scrupulous and joyful fidelity. But in Pavlova's dancing we are no longer aware of the conscious and painful obedience of the body to the dictates of a governing mind. It is as though the spirit itself had left its central citadel and, by some unwonted alchemy becoming dissolved in the blood and fibres of her being, had penetrated to the extremities of the limbs. Soul from body is no longer distinguishable, and which is servant to the other none can tell.

It goes without saying that her long and careful apprenticeship in the art of dancing has given Madame Pavlova perfect

proficiency in that technique of the ballet which is variously known as traditional, academic, or Italian. But although all dancing that is not grounded upon this technique is apt to become to a certain extent wavering and nerveless, it seems certain that this technique alone does not suffice for a dancer who dances with soul as well as body. After she had passed through her years of probation, Pavlova's individuality naturally began to assert itself, and she demanded a wider scope for the full expression of her emotions. This liberty she found in those gestures and poses, more naturally human than those of the conventional ballet, which had been discovered, or rather rediscovered, by Isadora Duncan, for they are native to the world of Greek art. The characteristic of her dancing, therefore, is the combination of the older traditional method with the freedom that is demanded for the expression of emotional ideas. Other dancers have sought to find this freedom by casting aside, or rather by never troubling to learn, the traditional technique. Pavlova knows well that the freedom of art is not to be attained by a wilful lawlessness, but only by a glad and strict submission to law. Thus she has carried the dance of the ballet a stage further along the lines of its natural evolution, not despising the heritage of the past, but enlarging it to meet the deeper needs of the present.

In particular, she has shown that true dancing demands the service of every member and particle of the body. No one is now so simple as to suppose that dancing is the business only, or even principally, of the legs and feet. Carlo Blasis, a hundred years ago, said that the position, the opposition, all the movements and carriage of the arms, are perhaps the most difficult parts of the dance; and Noverre still earlier remarked, "Peu d'artistes sont distingués par un beau style de bras." But the more subtly emotional the dance becomes, the more finely must be studied the play of light and shade over the whole surface of the body. Pavlova's dancing is as expressive in its minutest details as in its general lines. Her dance lives in her finger-tips. The character-play of her hands is astonishing. They take their part in the interpretation of the music; they are, as it were, illuminating appendices to the story of love and joy, of rapture and fear, that her body relates. Her face dances too. She has a command of vivid facial expression such as few actresses can equal. Never for an instant does she betray the least preoccupation with her steps. Her face is like a mirror, reflecting the passing lights and shadows of the music and the mood. The head dances, the eyes dance, the brow, the neck, the lips dance—the dance, in a word, penetrates her whole being, as the breeze penetrates the body of a tree to the least shuddering of the tiniest leaf.

Indeed in Pavlova's art is realised the full meaning of the dance, which is none other than the complete possession of the body by the spirit. I understood this best when I saw her, not in motion on the stage, but at rest in her home. Reclining in a chair, she sketched with a few inimitable gestures the *Danse des Papillons* . It was scarcely more than a turn of the head, a light in the eyes, a fluttering of the fingers, and yet the mood was evoked as surely as a painter in a few nervous strokes might capture an emotion and fix it on his canvas. In this almost intangible expression the dance seemed to become, if you will suffer the paradox, independent even of motion, rather a design living in the brain, an intellectual thing which could communicate itself by a hint, a breath, by an energy of the spirit rather than of the body.

The idea of the dance—the choregraphic design—is sometimes suggested to her by music, by fragments from the works of Delibes, Chopin, Tchaikovsky or Saint-Saëns; sometimes it is hinted in a chance sight or incident of everyday life; sometimes it springs into being independently of any external impulse, as spontaneously as a melody is conceived in the musician's or an image in the poet's mind. *Le Cygne* , which she dances to the music of Saint-Saëns, owed its origin to a walk with M. Fokine in a park in St Petersburg. Seeing some swans floating upon the water, M. Fokine remarked to Madame Pavlova that it would be easy for her with her supple and slender throat to take the graceful motion of the bird as the theme of one of her dances. Her figure has something of the easy dignity of the swan, and in the gliding motions, to the accompaniment of the cool music of Saint-Saëns, she is perhaps more at ease

PAVLOVA AND MORDKIN

Photograph: Foulsham & Banfield, Ltd.

than in those passages which demand a more stormy energy. In this dance she represents with singular beauty the proud carriage of that remote bird, its swooning death and its sudden collapse into lifelessness. It displays her skill in the difficult act of falling; she sinks to earth without any suggestion of arrangement or preparedness, ceasing to dance as swiftly and silently as a flame may cease to burn, her limbs failing her, as though her body had actually resigned its spirit.

Her interpretation of Strauss's *Blue Danube* is a perfect personification of the river-spirit. From beginning to end it sounds a clear note of joy and untrammelled life. Pavlova dances it in her freest style; the pirouette and the entrechat have no part in this simulation of the triumphing flood. All the phases of the river's moods live in her dancing—its strong, pulsating race in mid-torrent, its bursts of sky-flung spray, its quiet dalliance in secret, wood-browned pools, its gentle play with the entangling weeds, its smooth descents over the breasting rocks ending in a laughing and ecstatic tumult.

What expression Pavlova can obtain even in the narrower scope of the traditional school may be seen in one of her dances to a Chopin valse. She appears as a young girl on the night of her first ball, in a simple white frock, somewhat longer than the usual ballet-dancer's skirt. She is dancing the dreams of girlhood in the garden after the ball is ended, when suddenly the lover, to whom she has just lost her heart, appears on a balcony and throws her a rose. She gathers it to her breast and in her happy dance she lives over again those revealing moments when her heart suddenly blossomed into the life of love. Then looking up she blows a kiss to the balcony where her lover had stood. To her shy dismay she finds him still standing there, a witness to her confessed surrender. She is confused with a modest shame for what in her maiden innocence she fears must seem an unmaiden-like boldness. The surprised and delighted lover offers his proposal. After a moment of the most delicious embarrassment she fearfully nods her assent and skips away in a transport of excited joy. It is a delicate suggestion of the troubled and innocent emotions of first love, as suggestive in its rendering of that neutral and indefinite age that lies between girlhood and womanhood as a picture by Greuze.

But perhaps the most perfect of all Pavlova's dances is the *Papillons* . It has been said that she "does not so much imitate the movement of a butterfly as the emotional quality of a butterfly-flight, the sense raised in our minds by watching it; and then it is not an ordinary butterfly, nor a plain lepidopteron, but a Grimm butterfly, a dream butterfly, a butterfly multiplied many times by itself, raised as it were to the Pavlova-th power." With that sense of the elimination of weight which is characteristic of her dancing, Pavlova is able to suggest the grace of things flying, things swimming, things borne upon the breeze. The *Papillons* is the quintessence of the spirit of everything that dances in the wind, and is kissed by the sun, and has intrigues with the flowers, and lives its irresponsible life between the sunrise and sunset of a summer day. It appears to be danced almost wholly with the eyes and the finger-tips; the dancer is on the stage and off again all within the incredibly short space of thirty seconds. Yet she told me that, on account of its ceaseless vibrating motion, of all her dances it is the most exhausting.

But Pavlova's dancing is not limited to the expression merely of thistledown lightness and inconsequential gaiety; it has a deeper reach, and at times is borne upon a flood of passion. *L'Automne Bacchanale* is a stormy and tumultuous dance, affecting the mind like that vision which Keats saw in the "marble brede of men and maidens" on a Grecian urn:

"What men or gods are these? What maidens loth?
What mad pursuit? What struggle to escape?
What pipes and timbrels? What wild ecstasy?"

It was this dance which inspired Mr Holbrook Jackson's spirited eulogy. "She does not make you think of herself," he writes in his "Romance and Reality"; "she sets you dreaming of all the dancing that has ever been, of all the dancing that is. Whilst watching her I could not help thinking she was not merely following the rules of an art, but that she was following the rules of life. The leaves

PAVLOVA AND MORDKIN

Photograph: Foulsham & Banfield, Ltd.

dance in the breeze, the flowers dance in the sun, the worlds dance in space, and Pavlova dancing is a part of this cosmic measure.

"Everybody in the theatre must have felt something similar—especially when she and Michael Mordkin, her superb consort in the art, danced together the *Bacchanale* of Glazounov. I imagine also those dim segments of faces in the darkened auditorium, many of them reflecting the frigid morality of English respectability, would be touched to strange emotions. Their staid owners would feel a new wakefulness, recalling as in a dream all that had ever happened to them of passion or beauty, all that might have happened to them had they followed their real desires, their sacred whims.... The swaying form of Pavlova rhymed and romped with life and joy, with love and beauty. O the wild flight across the stage, the hot pursuit, the sweet dalliance, and then the rich luxury of surrender! The very essence of life was there: life so full of joy that it overflowed with blissful abandonment until it sank from the only pardonable excess —excess of happiness."

In this dance Pavlova has met the exponents of the modern "barefoot" school on their own ground, and,—shall we say? vanquished them. Her training in the strict traditional method has taught her that lesson, invaluable in all the arts, the restraint of emotion. For even in the *Bacchanale* there is restraint, the art that conceals art, else she could not have attained that perfect unison of rhythm which gives to the dance the swinging quality of a wave.

Pavlova may be said to have introduced impressionism into the dance, and so to have brought it into line with the tendencies of modern art. Not impressionism as Zola understood it—"merely an excuse for not taking pains." In this respect her faultless precision more resembles the fine work of a Dutch *genre* painting. But she is an impressionist in creating a sudden and brilliant effect without the appearance of laboured effort and without the addition of a superfluous touch, in presenting with an economy of swift gesture the firm outline of an incident, the essential summary of a scene, the breathing heart of an emotion. Although she flashes across the vision for no more than a few seconds, she nevertheless leaves in the mind the memory of a complete utterance, something perfectly finished, definite, precise, whole, like a clear-sounding lyric, or a finely-cut sculpture. For in her work, as in all true impressionism, there is nothing blurred; it is rapid, but it is just and sure; it goes to the roots; it ignores what is irrelevant and seizes on the essential. Actual mimicry has no place in her dance; she is not a copyist of nature; she embodies the salient moments, the vital energies, of beauty and passion.

But when all is said, nothing is said. She refuses to yield herself to analysis. Too swift for the eye, she altogether outpaces the pen. One can only repeat the words of that baffled interviewer who wisely wrote: "Pavlova can only be adequately understood by the person to whom she is an everlasting mystery—by the mind that cannot understand her. The man who feels he can, or thinks he can, or knows he can, sum her up in so many words; who fancies he has done his duty to her and to reason when he has declared that she is the finest dancer that he has ever seen in all his life; who says 'I have seen Pavlova' as a man would say 'I have seen the boat-race'—as if the whole thing were over and done with, and that nothing more was to be learned, or not learned, by another and another visit: such a man speaks without having felt.... She is uninterviewable— unphotographable—undrawable. But she is not uncaricaturable; for are not all the phrases of the pen and strokes of the pencil but caricatures that attempt to describe and picture perfection? And what is perfection but Pavlova?"

In the troupe which accompanied Madame Pavlova at the Palace Theatre in London there were several artistic performers, but one calls for special notice—Mademoiselle Schmolz. Her dancing in Glinka's "Mazurka" and Brahms' "Rhapsodie Hongroise" had all that lilt and swing and hint of devilry which, by every rule of the theatre at any rate, the dancing of half-barbaric peasants ought to have. A dance which she and Mademoiselle Plaskaweska danced to the most mischievously ironical of Chopin's waltzes was, I have no hesitation in saying, one of the most completely satisfying things

MADEMOISELLE SCHMOLZ

Photograph: Dover Street Studios, Ltd.

ever seen upon the stage. The credit belongs in part to Mikail Mordkin, who was the composer, but it is scarcely possible to conceive a more spirited interpretation than that given by the two executants. The theme was simply a petty squabble about a rose. One of the maidens covets the love-token which the other flaunts so provokingly; there follows a pretty wrangle on tiptoe, lively grimaces, and the trophy is wrested from its rightful owner. The latter now becomes the aggressor, displays a delightful petulance, and, between smiles and tears, pursues the laughing thief. The nosegay is won back, and then, just as your sympathy is becoming earnestly engaged in the alternations of triumph and despair, the rose is tossed upon the ground, and both minxes run away with mocking laughter, leaving you half aggrieved at having been fooled into a serious concern in their empty mischief. It is simple, trivial, silly if you like, and it is all over in half-a-minute—yet it prints on the mind a picture like one of those rare glimpses of incidents sometimes seen in real life, the memory of which goes with a man for half a lifetime.

Mikail Mordkin received his training in the same school as Anna Pavlova, that attached to the Marianski Theatre in St Petersburg. The two have been associated in a somewhat uneasy partnership at the Palace Theatre in London, and in the United States. Mordkin has achieved the distinction of being the only *danseur* who has ever found favour in America. There, as in England, before the coming of the Russians, the chief function of the man dancer was to rush out at the psychological moment and rescue the ballerina as she fell into his arms, with her eyes staring into the drops and one toe pointing upwards towards the limelight man. Apart from performing this useful service, on account of which he was tolerated as a kind of necessary nuisance, his part was almost a sinecure.

The performances of Mordkin, together with those of Nijinsky, have brought about a reversal of the somewhat contemptuous popular judgment upon male dancing, for undoubtedly the Anglo-Saxon public shared to some extent the prejudice of Southey, who said that every male dancer ought to be hamstrung. There is nothing of the twittering effeminacies of the proverbial "French dancing-master" in Mordkin's dancing; its main characteristic is manliness. His build is robust, massive, noble. His physical qualities undoubtedly leave some of his less critical admirers blind to the deficiencies of his art. His splendid physique is fortified by a course of rigorous and continual training. In addition to his daily exercise, it is not unusual for him to go to the theatre three hours before the performance begins and, without the accompaniment of music, to go through all the preliminary postures of the dance. Instead of becoming exhausted by this exercise, he is fit and eager for the ballet to begin.

Mordkin has shown that grace is not only consistent with true virility in dancing, but is indispensable to it. In their folk-dances the top-booted Russian dancers give a fine display of masculine vigour, but it is always upon the edge of the grotesque. The beauty of a man's strength is hidden rather than revealed by these spasms of violence; it is best seen in those lines, suggestive of sleeping force, which give to Mordkin's poses the heroic quality of Greek sculpture. His dancing is distinguished by its reserve. It always leaves something to the imagination. His gestures in the "Arrow Dance" derive no little of their effectiveness from what they suggest, but leave unsaid. It is the warrior not at war but at play, and like the gambolling of young tigers affects us by the passion that it only hints at. His dancing has a constant tendency to forsake motion for repose. In his entrechats and pirouettes I seemed to note a certain reluctance, as though they were a concession demanded by popular taste, or a lingering tradition of the ballet technique. Yet when motion is required, Mordkin can give it, and of the freest, most buoyant, most swinging quality. The reckless swing of the galloping entry in the *Automne Bacchanale* was magnificent. That was a dance of dances! The riot of wine, the sap of youth, the tumult of love, the sudden liberation of vigorous limbs, were all expressed in a rush of movement that was somehow curiously restrained, as the foaming progress of a wave is restrained, never tempted by excess of ecstasy into breaking the steady sweep of its own rhythm.

MIKAIL MORDKIN

Photograph: Foulsham & Banfield, Ltd.

A comparison of the art of Mordkin and Nijinsky would be almost ir-relevant. Their style differs just in the same degree as their physique. If Nijinsky is the winged Mercury of the dance, Mordkin is the Apollo. Nijinsky's is the dancing of motion, Mordkin's of repose; the temper of the one is volatile, of the other equable and restrained; wit, gaiety, elegance, ebullience of youthful spirits, are the characteristics of the younger dancer; dignity, power, and a slumbering passion, of the elder. The hint of Puck-like fancy is entirely absent in Mordkin's performances; his dramatic qualities are less elastic than Nijinsky's, his personality less various, more rigidly settled in a definite mould.

While other Russian dancers pass with meteoric flight across the English stage, Madame Lydia Kyasht burns like a fixed star of all but the first magnitude. Discerning critics observed her with pleasure behind the footlights of the Empire Theatre for the first time one autumn evening in 1908. She had been summoned from Russia to dance in London for four weeks,—she has been dancing there for three years and her engagement has still two more to run. Her position as *première danseuse* in an English ballet has both its advantages and its dangers. Appearing in a ballet that is really very little more than a ballet of amateurs, she achieves without great difficulty the effect desired I suppose by every ballet-dancer,—that of a visitant from some more gracious and ethereal sphere. She trips where her companions tramp. She alone has wings. Yet, although her art profits by the contrast, it suffers from the isolation. It is difficult for her to keep it keyed to its highest pitch when she is deprived of the stimulus of criti-cism and emulation. Moreover, as there is no competent master of the ballet to compose for her, she is compelled to be her own choregrapher, and the work of composition demands a different order of intelligence from that of the executant. Yet in spite of these unfavourable conditions, the character of her dancing remains remarkably pure. If it lacks the dazzling executive brilliance of her former fellow-pupils, Pavlova and Karsavina, it is marked by a certain statuesque dignity which is somewhat notable in a ballerina. Even a great dancer may have arresting attitudes but fail to connect them. Lydia Kyasht passes from attitude to attitude in a single continuous sequence of admirable poses which flow one into another without a pause and without a flaw. Her purity of line is never broken by one of those inartistic feats of athletic dexterity which sometimes disfigure the dancing of Adeline Genée. She invariably resists the besetting temptation of a clever dancer to let accomplishment trespass upon grace. Unfortunately the good fairy who has endowed her with so many gifts appears to have withheld the greatest of them all—imagination. Finish and refinement can never make amends for the absence of mood. At times her dancing leaves us so cold that we are persuaded that she is dancing with her head but not with her heart.

It is worth while remarking that when any Russian dancer appears in England or America, she is almost invariably described as the "première danseuse of the Russian Imperial Ballet." This denomination is vague, and usually inaccurate. Theoretically there can be only two *ballerine assolute* in all the Russias—one in St Petersburg and one in Moscow. As a matter of fact, in St Petersburg at the present moment both Kschesinskaya and Preobrajenskaya hold this rank, although of the two, the former is granted precedence. The latter has now nominally retired, but she continues to make six or eight appearances every season. Madame Kschesinskaya has never performed in England. She once visited London privately, but when she found that an engagement there would necessitate appearing nightly, she declared that such a task was "blood-drying work," and fled incontinently to Russia. In the Russian capital she herself chooses the occasions when she deigns to appear. The *ballerina assoluta* of Moscow is Mademoiselle Catrina Geltzer, who has recently appeared at the Alhambra. Madame Pavlova belongs to the grade known as *ballerina* , or *première danseuse* , the next below that of *ballerina assoluta* . She is marked out to succeed to the place vacated by Madame Preobrajenskaya in the supreme rank in the hierarchy. Madame Karsavina and Mademoiselle Balashova are at present equal in degree to Madame Pavlova. Madame Lydia Kyasht is in Russia still only *première sujet* .

LYDIA KYASHT
Photograph: Ellis & Walery

CHAPTER XII

THE ENGLISH BALLET

I N a retrospect of the performances of the Russians in London this year, a correspondent of *The Times* summed up the effect of their achievement upon the state of mind of the spectator of the English ballet in these words: "This summer of 1911 has brought more than an æsthetic revolution with it: in bringing the Russian ballet to Covent Garden it has brought a positively new art, it has extended the realm of beauty for us, discovered a new continent, revealed new faculties and means of salvation in ourselves. Alas! many pleasant illusions have been shattered thereby, many idols have tumbled from their pedestals; we have grown up terribly fast and lost the power of enjoying things that pleased our callow fancies a year or two ago. Who can go back now with the old zest to the robust vivacity of X or the amateurish *minauderies* of Y? Who will put up any longer with the battered themes, the insipid music, the ingenious setting, and the clumsy grouping to which we were accustomed once? They will still have their public, those things; they will serve for entertainment, for stuffing to that pillow on which the backbone of the British nation leans till bedtime; but they will no longer do for the 'seven hundred honest folk' who seek at that hour for the means to 'make their souls.'"

Although I cannot claim to be one of the honest folk who go to the Empire at that hour "to make their souls," it was nevertheless somewhat dismayedly that, with the rhythm of the Russians still marching through the brain, I once again witnessed a ballet fairly representative of the modern English type. We were no longer in the atmosphere of art, but in the atmosphere of commerce. The peculiarity of the atmosphere of commerce is that it leaves nothing to the imagination, and therefore it leaves the imagination cold. "The art of the pen," said Meredith in the person of one of the characters of his novels, "is to rouse the inward vision, instead of labouring with a drop-scene brush, as if it were to the eye." The English ballet is not content with the primitive simplicity of a drop-scene brush; it labours with a host of mechanical devices—with extravagant properties, with photographic scenery, with the stratagems of electricians, with all the means that the stage manager can array to dissuade the inward vision from rousing itself. Its aim apparently is to create a diversion for the eye so that the imagination may slumber undisturbed. The stage as a rule is so crowded, that any suggestion of a governing design is lost in a general bewildering flicker of motion like that of the cinematograph. Frequently the *corps de ballet* have no room for any more elaborate step than an artless hop and a right-about turn, a kind of convalescent pirouette. Perhaps it is as well—safety may sometimes lie in numbers. "What has come to us," asked Professor Selwyn Image a dozen years ago *apropos* of the *Butterflies* ballet, "that we are all gone crazy over crowds and jumble and properties and frippery?"

A strange circumstance is that the English ballet not infrequently has the air of being discontented with its enforced silence. At its best the ballet is not the translation of words into gesture: it is the translation, or rather the transposition of life into gesture. It is the presentment to eye and ear by means of rhythmic motion and pictorial design, of a certain feeling about life, of certain moods and visions which have never crystallised into words. "It begins and ends," it has been well said, "before words have formed themselves, in a deeper consciousness than that of speech." To think of ballet merely as dumb show is the same as to think of painting merely as illustration. It exists as the supplement rather than as the substitute of words. It does not merely tell a story; it tells it, or rather it should tell it, in a way in which words alone could not tell it. It tells it with a beauty which, we will not say is greater than, but is at any rate different from, the beauty of words. But the ballet of commerce, aiming at literalness rather than suggestion,

LYDIA KYASHT

IN *Sylvia*

seems strangely handicapped by its speechlessness. It appears to be groping for the libretto. It does not tell a story so much as suggest that it has a story to tell, which it would, if it could, impart to the spectator. Probably because they never seek to go outside the narrow circle of conventionalised gestures, which the English ballet has received as a sacred tradition from the Italian, the performers have the air of attempting to communicate with one another in the deaf and dumb language of a mute, or rather of one who wilfully deprives himself of the use of his tongue. The feeling that they arouse in the spectator is one almost of impatience, as with the folly of a man who uses a finger alphabet when he might just as well talk rationally.

In speaking of the English ballet, Mr Max Beerbohm has gaily admitted his inability to master the meaning of formalised gesture: "When a ballerina lays the palms of her hands against her left cheek, and then snatching them away, regards them with an air of mild astonishment, and then swaying slightly backwards, touches her forehead with her finger-tips, and then suddenly extends both arms above her head, I ought of course to be privy to her inmost meaning. I ought to have a thorough grasp of her exact state of mind. Friends have often explained to me, with careful demonstrations, the significance of the various gestures that are used in the ballet—and these gestures are not very many—and I have more than once committed them to memory, hoping that though I could never be illuded, I might at least be not bemused. But, after all this trouble, the next ballet that I have seen has teased and puzzled me as unkindly as ever. Is it that gestures were given to the ballerina to conceal her thoughts? Or is it merely that the quickness of the hand deceives the eye?"

One of the criteria of the ballet is the quality of its silence. In the perfect ballet the silence is never apprehended as a negation or a deficiency, any more than it is in a painting or a statue. The interpolation of words would indeed be felt to be an impertinence. Where the rhythm is entirely satisfying, the mind is content. Not the least of the merits of the Russian ballet is this quality of completeness in its silence. There are some exceptions: at times the action of *Le Pavillon d'Armide* stumbles and seems to cry for speech; but in *Le Spectre de la Rose* would not a single spoken word break the spell? The gestures of the dancers are never drawn from that limited stock of conventions which Mr Beerbohm tried in vain to memorise, which are in fact a kind of stock-in-trade, and can be borne in mind and applied at will like the commonplaces of the newspaper leader-writers; they are fluid and variable and flow naturally out of the emotion. They are in fact gestures, and not, as they usually are in the English ballet, gesticulations.

But there is good reason to believe that the English ballet is on the eve of a renaissance. The success of the Russians must have taught the managers that a gorgeous spectacle is not really necessary for the delight of the public,—in the Russian repertory probably the simplest ballets were the most appreciated. Already in the *Dance Dream* the Alhambra has produced a ballet which, if the theme was insipid, at any rate had the crowning virtue of breadth and simplicity of treatment. A sense of space was created; the tumult of action was varied by passages of sobriety; an effect of beauty was produced, larger and serener than any that has been seen in the English ballet during recent years. The principals of course were Russians—Mademoiselle Balashova succeeded Mademoiselle Geltzer as *première danseuse* —but the performance of the English dancers showed that under proper handling they are capable of better things than the pantomime displays to which they have been used to be restricted.

The English ballet still awaits the coming of the great English dancer—it is too early yet to know whether Miss Phyllis Bedells will be she—but now that public interest is at last wide awake the primary condition of the creation of a native school of ballet is satisfied.

But there is one dancer of genius, whom, if the English stage has not produced, it at any rate monopolises. It has become difficult to think of Madame Adeline Genée as belonging to any other country than England, nevertheless the conscientious annalist must record, however unwillingly, the fact that she was born at Aarhus, in Denmark. If she was not born dancing, she danced almost from her cradle. At the age of eight she began that

ALEXANDRA BALASHOVA

arduous course of training which forms the solid groundwork of her art. She was instructed by her uncle, Alexander Genée. She also profited greatly by the strict supervision of her aunt, who, it is interesting to note, was a Hungarian. If, indeed, there be any natural magic in the dancing of the natives of Eastern Europe, it must have passed into Genée's style long before the Russian dancers were heard of in this country. Her aunt was her most vigorous and helpful critic; when she pleased her audiences she was glad, but when she pleased this exacting connoisseur she was content. Madame Genée made her first appearance at the Opera House at Copenhagen; at the age of sixteen she was dancing at the Royal Theatre in Berlin, from whence she proceeded to Munich. It was there that she received that telegram which may be said to have determined her subsequent career—the invitation to take the position of *première danseuse* for six weeks at the Empire Theatre, London.

She made her début in England in *Monte Cristo* , in November 1897. She has remained the popular favourite of the English public ever since, and perhaps not of the English public only, but of the American also. Amid the crowd of dancers of all nationalities she has maintained her pride of place. In *Vineland* her dancing first seemed to attain its full brilliance. Then followed the *Milliner Duchess* and *High Jinks* , the latter notable for the famous hunting scene in which the verve and spirit of her dancing won all hearts. Finally came Delibes' *Coppelia* , an example of the classic ballet at its best. *Coppelia* was to Genée what *La Sylphide* was to Taglioni, *Giselle* to Grisi, and *Eoline* to Lucille Grahn. Naturally it is, as she told me, her favourite ballet. But perhaps her triumph in the *Dryad* was even greater. It gave her an opportunity for displaying not only her marvellous technique, but also a perhaps half-unsuspected power of raising and expressing emotion. It afforded scope for the range of her feeling and revealed the actress beneath the dancer. In the first scene she comes out of the tree trunk in which the jealousy of Aphrodite has imprisoned her. Once a year she is allowed to roam abroad and delight in the sunlight and the flowers and the breeze. Her heart is on fire with joy at all the sights and sounds about her; but a still greater joy is in store for her—she meets a shepherd who falls in love with her. She relates her story to him in gestures which are as explicit as speech, and tells him he must go away and return at the end of ten years—she delightfully counts out the tale of years on the flowers she has gathered. If throughout the ten years he is faithful to her she will be released. The ten years pass, and on an autumn evening she comes out of her tree prison once again. Will he come? She is sure of it and dances for joy. Will he come? She searches for him eagerly through the meadows and down the glades. Will he come? Troubling doubts assail her, and her eyes begin to fill with despair. Will he come? Of course he will. She is still rippling and glowing with joy. She hears his voice. He is singing the old familiar love song. He is there, and on his arm is a human shepherdess to whom he is singing the song that once was only hers. The faithless lover and his new-found love pass through the meadow and down the glade, and then the Dryad, forsaken and forlorn, turns to the sheltering trunk in which she can hide herself and her despair.

The fable is slender as a fairy tale, yet it gave Genée the chance of showing that she could pass from one emotion to another with the same rapidity, ease and expressiveness that mark her steps. She was by turns elfish, tender, sad, merry, passionate or despairing. In the first moments after escaping from the imprisoning tree, her dancing was full of that quality which so often inspires it—the spirit of the eternal child.

But the first and foremost quality of Madame Genée's dancing is its technical perfection. If there is such a thing as a physical genius for the dance, independent of the qualities of the spirit, that genius is hers. She reveals it in the mere act of walking across the room. There is a brilliance in her movement, a resiliency in her tread, that distinguishes her from all other women. If the ancients were right in attributing four elements to the composition of the body, one would say that hers was compounded solely of air and fire. But whereas many dancers might have relied almost entirely on this natural genius, which is hers by right of birth, Genée has added to it a training which in severity, conscientiousness

ADELINE GENÉE

and thoroughness perhaps few dancers have equalled. For years she has spent four hours a day in front of her huge mirror practising her steps, usually under the careful supervision of her uncle. "I have given my life and myself to my dancing," she says, and the words are true in a very special and literal sense. She has served her art with almost the rigour of asceticism. She avoids wine. She eats sparely. She shuns a supper-party. When her work is over her day is done, and she drives from the theatre home to bed. She has fulfilled to the letter Ruskin's affirmation that an artist must submit to a law which it was painful to obey, in order that she may bestow a delight which it is gracious to bestow.

In proficiency in the strict, classical school of ballet-dancing, it is possible that Madame Genée has never been surpassed and perhaps not even equalled. Within these limits her work is faultless. Every detail is sedulously studied, and is executed with accuracy and ease. The position of the fingers, the lines of the arabesque, the resumption of the exact attitude at the end of no matter how many and how rapid pirouettes—everything is as exact as if it had been drawn by an artist with infinite leisure for correction, instead of executed in the heat of the moment without an instant's pause between one movement and the next. Every step has its name; every gesture belongs to its code; there is one way and no other of executing them rightly, and that way is Madame Genée's. But the dance is too rapid and too flowing to be dissected into its constituent parts. The connoisseur recognises them and knows that the apparent spontaneity is obtained only by the mastery of a science as strict as mathematics; the spectator uneducated in the dance remarks the general effect of beauty, and is instinctively aware that the performance has something of the qualities of a masterpiece of art. But this extreme physical sureness and dexterity is not without its dangers. The dancer is tempted to exhibit mere *tours de force* which a less proficient performer would be saved by her very incompetence from attempting, and the temptation is the greater through the knowledge that these are the accomplishments which call forth the most tempestuous applause from a public that cares less for the beautiful than for the marvellous. In a recent divertissement, *A Dream of Butterflies and Roses* , no movement, not even the magnificent circles made backwards with wide flying steps, excited the audience to such a pitch of enthusiasm as one particularly trying piece of gymnastic—a slow rising from the ground on one pointed toe. But Genée's mastery of technique is so complete that the least hint of strain is eliminated and even this somewhat acrobatic feat was almost transformed into a delightful flow of grace. The ease with which she overcomes technical difficulties creates a delight of its own, cheating one's fears, and compelling an admission of beauty where one had dreaded to see only athletic prowess.

To this technical perfection Genée adds certain spiritual qualities which are all her own. As I have said, the *Dryad* revealed a dramatic ability which had been perhaps overlooked in the admiration of her pure dancing. This capacity for pantomime would probably have been earlier appreciated if the ballets at the Empire had allowed it more scope. But the peculiar note of her spirit is an abounding gaiety, as clear and elemental as that of a child, affecting the heart like vital and exhilarating laughter. There is a kind of arch-merriment in her dancing which seems to flow out of the pure exultation of movement, at times almost threatening to break through the restraints of technique and convert the dance into a romp. But the elasticity of the dance is always great enough to meet the freest ebullience of spirits; there is, as it were, no leakage of vitality; every atom of force is spent in steps and movements that never lose their precision and exactitude. Genée's dancing refutes those detractors who assert

that the academic style of the ballet is a fatal limitation to the artist's freedom of expression. She shows that, when it is brought to the perfection
to which she has developed it, it is fluent and elastic enough to express
the extremes of, at any rate, the more volatile emotions. The hunting
dance in *High Jinks* carries the dance as far in the direction of high spirits,
of exhilaration unmixed with passion, of sheer delight in the physical fact
of life, as it can possibly go. The spirited little horsewoman in the black
riding-habit, that clings closely to the lines of her gay and lithe

ADELINE GENÉE

Photograph: Dover Street Studios, Ltd.

figure, has an air at once of fragility and vigour; she is borne through the air on her dashing leaps, she curvets, she caracoles, the slender steely limbs make nothing of the weighty burden of the skirt and boots—and yet it is all done with such a whirl and wind of enthusiasm that the motive force appears to be not muscular activity but merely a fever of the blood. All the jollity, all the glorious high spirits, all the high-heartedness, all the intoxication of delight, in all the hunting mornings that ever were, are concentrated in that swaying, swirling, leaping, laughing figure.

There is something essentially of the North in Genée's dancing, a freshness and energy like that of the north wind, a hint of the athlete in the vigorous clean-limbed movements, an absence of passion, a purity, shall we say a coldness? Her spirit seems to belong to the heights rather than to the depths. It is bright rather than subtle. It is full of high lights but lacking in half-tones.

Although "finish" in a technical sense is the peculiar characteristic of Genée's art, it is not marked by those almost indefinable nuances which give the dance, no less than the painting or the poem, a quality with which not even the finest workmanship can endow it. These refinements belong to the region not of the intelligence but of the spirit, and cannot be laid hold of by analysis. They depend upon a very delicate perception, upon a subtle responsiveness to the rhythm of life. Underlying the precision of her work is a kind of crudity. There is no mood of creative beauty. The outline is firm rather than tender. The emotional qualities of the dance are explicit, simple and wholesome, but they are never subtle, nor do they appear to be nourished by a great depth of spirit. We miss the suggestion of those moods that are elemental and incalculable. There is a gladness that cannot show itself in frolicsomeness, and there is an ecstasy too near to tears to have any likeness to high spirits. Perfect within its own domain, we feel that beyond the frontiers of her art lie tracts of the spirit unexplored.

To Adeline Genée England in particular owes a debt greater than to any other dancer. It was she who continued, or rather restored, the tradition of the great dancing of the earlier half of the last century. She aroused enthusiasm for the ballet in an age when that enthusiasm had grown cold. She helped to put an end to a perverted form of dancing. Her example shone out with a clear light in that thick darkness just before the dawn, and for more than a decade she remained true to her ideals through good report and ill. It is safe to say that when the devotees of many other deities of the dance have ceased to kindle their tapers, her own shrine will always be brightly illuminated.

Mr Max Beerbohm has paid her a notable tribute, which has all the more value seeing that he confesses that for him the ballet has no meaning. "No monstrous automaton is that young lady," he said, writing of her performance in *Coppelia* in 1906. "Perfect though she be in the 'haute école,' she has by some miracle preserved her own self. She was born a comedian and a comedian she remains, light and liberal as foam. A mermaid were not a more surprising creature than she—she of whom one half is as that of an authentic ballerina, whilst the other is that of a most intelligent, most delightfully human actress. A mermaid were, indeed, less marvellous in our eyes. She would not be able to diffuse any semblance of humanity into her tail. Madame Genée's intelligence seems to vibrate in her very toes. Her dancing, strictliest classical though it is, is a part of her acting. And her acting, moreover, is of so fine a quality that she makes the old ineloquent conventions of gesture tell their meanings to me, and tell them so exquisitely that I quite forget my craving for words.... Taglioni in *Les Arabesques* ? I suspect, in my heart of hearts, she was no better than a doll. Grisi in *Giselle* ? She may, or may not, have been passable. Genée! It is a name our grandchildren will cherish, even as we cherish now the names of those bygone dancers. And alas! our grandchildren will never believe, will never be able to imagine, what Genée was."

Is there a young English dancer of promise who will one day vindicate the honour of England and succeed to the place which Genée now triumphantly holds in the popular favour? Miss Phyllis Bedells is a possible candidate for fame. She has recently taken the principal rôle in *Sylvia* at the Empire in the absence of Madame

231

Kyasht, but she danced more happily in her original subordinate part. Her dancing has a charm which in some measure is enhanced by its very faultiness. It is the charm of immaturity, the suggestion of the delightful gambolling of a young animal at play. Her training, so far as it goes, has been painstaking, but what chiefly distinguishes her performance from the routine work of the average English dancer is an unaffected zest, almost a vividness of delight, which the obvious troublesomeness of the technique is unable to depress. The main difference between the would-be dancer and the born dancer is that the dance of the former is always the repetition of a lesson, whereas every dance of the latter is like a new creation. So far as it is already possible to judge, Miss Bedells belongs to the latter class.

If the English ballet has yet produced no native ballerina worthy to rank with the great Continental dancers, the absence of a male dancer of any distinction is still more remarkable. An exception can scarcely be made in favour of Mr Fred Farren, who fills the dual rôle of *premier danseur* and *maître de ballet* at the Empire. Neither as a composer of dances nor as an executant has he created anything that calls for special notice. His most successful achievement has been an adaptation of the French Apache dance. *La Valse Chaloupée* was originated, or rather popularised, by Max Dearly and Mademoiselle Mistinguette, a dancer who has brought into the dance all the nervous excitement of modernity. In introducing the Apache dance into *A Day in Paris* at the Empire, Mr Farren modified its more *outré* characteristics and at the same time gave it a more deeply passionate and dramatic significance. His able partner, Miss Beatrice Collier, imported into it a note of human tragedy that was more moving than the mere devilry of Mistinguette.

Probably the real reason why England has failed to produce a great school of ballet is principally owing to the absence of a *maître de ballet* of genius. The late Madame Katti Lanner and Madame Cavalazzi both possessed a thorough knowledge of technique, and were capable of designing dances that were suited to the capacities of their pupils; but their ideas were limited and their imagination feeble. There is no reason in the nature of things why English dancers should not rise to the same level of excellence as those of St Petersburg or Moscow. Probably the material is there, but the artist who can mould it into a design of the highest plastic beauty is lacking.

The dancer, after all, is very much in the position of a pawn in the game. She can provide an individual note of fine quality and tone, but it requires the genius of a master to provide the orchestration. The ballet is perhaps more responsive to the attitude of the public than any other branch of art, and the absence of a public seriously and critically interested in the dance has doubtless been responsible for the fact that the ballet has failed to attract the energies of men of talent. The priority of Russia in the art of the ballet is due above all else to that atmosphere which England lacks, an atmosphere of keen and enlightened criticism, of understanding sympathy and serious interest, among the public at large no less than among the artists themselves. That this is a condition absolutely essential to the success of the ballet is clearly shown in an instructive passage by the writer whom I have quoted at the beginning of this chapter.

Speaking of the excellence of the Russians he says:

"This sort of perfection in an art is the result of a long process. The artists are not only trained to it; they are born to it. The same names occur again and again in the history of the ballet; sons and daughters follow the calling of their parents, and find themselves wives and husbands among their fellow-dancers. Their limbs exist only for grace and suppleness, and are never stiffened by any other use. All their lives are devoted to dancing; and it is the constant occupation of their minds. A ballet-master is not an accident or sport of nature, but one who is acknowledged by his comrades to excel them in the sort of imagination in which they all share. A certain Russian, living in St Petersburg, was frequently puzzled by the strange behaviour of the guests in a flat across the street. An aged lady lived there, and once or twice a week she held receptions, and the strangest leapings and gyrations could be dimly seen through the curtains. In the end the aged lady

proved to be Mademoiselle P., the once famous dancer and daughter of another famous dancer, and these were her friends from the Corps de Ballet who came to take tea with her; they were merely talking 'shop,' and incidentally illustrating their ideas by showing each other various steps. Monsieur K., the ballet-master, composes ballets as he walks, and is watched by suspicious policemen swaying and waving his arms, while he goes absent-mindedly along the streets. When the Russian ballet was in Vienna, the guests in a certain hotel were roused more than once in the middle of the night by a heavy bumping and clatter from the room above. 'It is all right,' one of the dancers explained to a nervous stranger, 'it is evidently K. composing a ballet.' An idea had occurred to him in bed; and as Strauss, the waltz-maker, in those circumstances used to jump out to note a tune on his tablets, so Monsieur K. had to jump out and dance it. Undistracted by other things, a ballet-master goes about the world gathering all the scattered beautiful gestures, the nice correlations of innumerable details (and how the tilt of the chin or the pathos of a smile just crowns the perfection of an attitude of Pavlova's or Karsavina's!), and keeps them ready to issue, in organic order, from his mind at the inspiration of the appropriate musical phrase."

It is to be feared that the English ballet-dancer does not take herself sufficiently seriously. It may even be that she is a little ashamed of herself. One has the uneasy feeling that she regards dancing as merely a stepping-stone to higher things—to musical comedy for instance! It is her profession, not her art. Not until English dancers begin to realise the significance of the dance as art and to create that choregraphic atmosphere

which at present appears to exist only in Russia, shall we have a true renaissance of the Ballet in England.

BEATRICE COLLIER AND FRED FARREN
IN *La Danse des Apaches*
Photographs: Ellis & Walery

CHAPTER XIII

ORIENTAL AND SPANISH DANCING

I T does not require a very minute observation to discover that peoples are distinguished not only by their speech, but by their habitual movements and attitudes. Every country has its special unspoken idiom of gesture, which sometimes differs in different parts of the same country as perceptibly as the spoken dialect. This characteristic gesture is the foundation of every national dance, which does but elaborate and adorn it.

The composers of the Russian ballets have achieved novel and interesting effects by using this racial attitude as the basis for the scheme of some of their dances. In *Cléopâtre* they have adopted the attitude of the ancient Egyptians, or rather those attitudes which are depicted on the pottery and frescoes of the old Egyptian civilisation. Whether these attitudes were ever really typical of the attitudes of the people is at least questionable. It is quite as likely that they were an artistic convention of the time, due to the naïve conceptions of the draughtsman. But there can be no doubt that ancient Egypt had a characteristic alphabet of gesture, as individual as that of ancient Greece, although probably it has been exaggerated in the designs on the figured monuments by the faultiness of the perspective. This circumstance, however, does not render it any the less serviceable as an element of design in the dance. In *Scheherazade* , again, Nijinsky's dance is based upon the abrupt, angular, almost apish movements of the negro.

With Italians gesticulation so inevitably accompanies speech that it is not surprising that the ballet should have been originated and perfected, at all events so far as its pantomime is concerned, in Italy. Of course, as a people becomes more intellectual, and learns to express all the nuances of thought by means of language alone, it relies less upon the elucidation of gesture. Anglo-Saxons are naturally schooled in reserve and seek to avoid any betrayal of the emotions by physical expression. The national gesture nevertheless exists and finds its embodiment in the national dance, the Morris. America can scarcely be said to have any national dance, unless it be the cake walk, which is plainly stamped with all the ungainliness of ne-gro movement. But American vaudeville artists—I am thinking of some who have danced this year in London—seem almost unconsciously to have seized upon the American gesture and realised it in their dances. Naturally they have distorted it; they have given it the immoderate energy of American life, the exaggeration of American wit, and the sensational-ism of American advertisement. Who knows but that they will end by giving America its national dance!

The lines of bodily movement in the West are radically different from those of the East. The quality of action in the West is energy and abrupt-ness; it tends to express itself in angles rather than in curves. The gesture of the East moves with the lethargy, the subtlety, interrupted by sudden bursts of violence, that are characteristic of the Eastern temper. Nothing could be less suitable to the tranquillity and torpor of the East than the swift and intricate dances of more bracing climes. It may be affirmed as a rough generalisation that Western dancing gives the greater importance to the feet, Eastern dancing to the body. In many of the most characteristic Oriental dances, the body revolves around its own axis, as it were, while the legs remain stationary. Equally with the motions of the body, the Eastern dance has made extraordinary use of the motions of the hands

and arms. It has found an invaluable auxiliary in the extreme refinement
of the Eastern woman's hands, which always seem so infinitely more expressive than the passive oval mask of her face. For me the eternal, the
essential gesture of the East is symbolised in the movement of a woman's
hand that I saw through the iron grating of a koubba on the edge of the
Sahara—for where the Arab is, there is the East. The woman herself I did
not see, for she was

crouching upon the floor against the tomb. But her whole body could not have expressed her character more revealingly than her hand, with its fingers stained at the tips with henna to a bright orange colour and as astonishingly slender as those of a Madonna in a primitive Italian painting. I think I should scarcely be believed if I tried to tell how much there was of resignation, how much of a refined voluptuousness, in its delicate gesture.

Eastern dances, performed by really skilled Eastern dancers, have not yet been seen upon the European stage. Of course the Ouled-Nails and the hired *almées* of the Algerian cafés introduced the *danse du ventre* to Paris at the time of the first Exhibition. It would be easy to dismiss this dance with contempt if one had not seen it danced with a certain barbaric sincerity, far away from the atmosphere of cigarettes and liqueurs of the cafés of Biskra and Tunis. After all, a dance is very much like the Spanish inn of the olden days—you find in it principally what you bring to it. And so acute an observer as Lady Duff Gordon found in the *danse du ventre* an intensity that gave it a kind of dignity. "I could not call it voluptuous," she says, "any more than Racine's *Phèdre* ; it is Venus 'tout entière à sa proie attachée,' and to me it seemed tragic. It is far more realistic than the fandango and far less coquettish, because the thing represented is *au grand sérieux* , not travestied, *gazé* , or played with."

But the dancing of the East, or rather of India in particular, has found a very skilled translator in a dancer of American origin, Miss Ruth St Denis. I believe it is true that Miss St Denis has never actually been in India, but she has mixed freely with Indians; she has studied their art, their religions, their character, she has penetrated into the spirit of the people as far as it is possible for a Westerner to do so. She has, in fact, caught the gesture of the East. Her dancing has for the most part a religious and symbolic character—for it should be remembered that, besides the dances founded upon the passions, the East has evolved a whole range of dances illustrative of philosophical ideas. Buddhism has carried the symbolism of the body to an extraordinary degree of refinement. The locking and unfolding of the feet, the uplifting of the arms and the hands, even the very curves of the fingers, have all their esoteric meaning. The system of symbolism has so penetrated the actions of the dance that not infrequently the sequence and shades of the dancer's movements are unintelligible to an uninstructed eye. Thus the slow dance movements which Hindus contemplate with delight for hours, though they may appear drearily monotonous to the European, are full of instruction to the initiated. The ritual of the dance is almost as intimately connected with Buddhism as the simpler ritual of the altar with Catholicism. The wealthier temples possess trained bands of dancers, a sort of vestal virgins, known as Devadassis, the slaves of the god. They have the happy and pious custom of dancing twice daily before the images of the gods, once in propitiation of their own sins, once in intercession for the sins of the world. It is the posturing of the Devadassi, rather than the dancing of the more voluptuous Bayadère, that Miss Ruth Denis has sought to reproduce.

In her physical qualities, Miss St Denis is well fitted to represent the type of the East. While her beauty has much of the allure of sex, it has also that childish character which seems peculiar to the women of the East. Her figure is exquisitely slender and her arms are as supple, her hands as refined, as those of a Hindu. The way was prepared for her to a certain extent by the success which Miss Isadora Duncan had already achieved, and when she gave a series of fashionable matinées in New York in 1906, previous to her descent upon Europe, her recognition was immediate.

When she appeared at the Scala Theatre in London in 1908, Miss Ruth St Denis was accompanied by half-a-dozen natives, who supplied a note of human colour to the pictures of the street, the palace and the temple, which formed the background of her dances. In most of the scenes, the mystic atmosphere was assisted by the subdued light, the odour of incense and the native melodies embodied in the striking music of Herr Walter Meyrowitz. Her performances took the form of brief acts, illustrative of native life.

The Cobra Dance was, strictly speaking, not a dance at all, for it was performed in sitting, crouching or kneeling postures. The dancer appeared in the rôle of a snake-charmer, and throwing off

245

her mantle revealed her arms clasped over either shoulder, like two coiling snakes. On the first and fourth fingers of each hand two enormous emeralds gleamed like serpents' eyes. The arms slowly unwound and with a curiously sinuous motion began to writhe about her body. They twined, coiled, fought and darted with lightning flashes in all directions, simulating the movements of the reptile with astonishing fidelity. It was a marvellous exercise in the flexibility of the arms.

The Dance of the Spirit of Incense was set in a scene representing the women's quarter of an Indian house. The dancer entered bearing aloft a bowl of smoking incense. With solemn, hierophantic gestures she kindled the two censers that were placed on either side of the stage, and, as the smoke curled upwards, she danced gravely and slowly, all the motions of her body subtly responding to the rhythm of the wreathing smoke and flowing so imperceptibly one into another that they seemed less a sequence of separate movements than a single continuous thrill passing from the feet to the finger-tips.

But it was in the Nautch and the Temple Dances that Miss St Denis really established her claim to rank as a dancer of the first order. Clad in a dress of vivid green spangled with gold, her wrists and ankles encased in chattering silver bands, surrounded by the swirling curves of a gauze veil, the dancer passed from the first slow languorous movements into a vertiginous whirl of passionate delirium. Alluring in every gesture, for once she threw asceticism to the winds, and yet she succeeded in maintaining throughout that difficult distinction between the voluptuous and the lascivious. The mystic Dance of the Five Senses was a more artificial performance and only in one passage kindled into the passion of the Nautch. As the goddess Radha, she is dimly seen seated cross-legged behind the fretted doors of her shrine. The priests of the temple beat gongs before the idol and lay their offerings at her feet. Then the doors open, and

Radha descends from her pedestal to suffer the temptation of the five senses. The fascination of each sense, suggested by a concrete object, is shown forth in the series of dances. Jewels represent the desire of the sight, of the hearing the music of bells, of the smell the scent of flowers, of the taste wine, and the sense of touch is fired by a kiss. Her dancing was inspired by that intensity of sensuous delight which is refined to its furthest limit probably only in the women of the East. She rightly chose to illustrate the delicacy of the perceptions not by abandon but by restraint. The dance of touch, in which every bend of the arms and of the body described the yearning for the unattainable, was more freely imaginative in treatment. And in the dance of taste there was one triumphant passage, when, having drained the wine-cup to the dregs, she burst into a dionysiac nautch, which raged ever more wildly until she fell prostrate under the maddening influence of the god of wine. Then by the expression of limbs and features showing that the gratification of the senses leads to remorse and despair, and that only in renunciation can the soul realise the attainment of peace, she returns to her shrine and the doors close upon the seated image, resigned and motionless. So she affirmed in choice and explicit gesture the creed of the Buddha.

The art of Miss St Denis is not free from adventitious elements. It is too much concerned with the expression of ideas to give itself up wholly to the creation of beauty. It is symbolic, but not in the large, suggestive way in which Isadora Duncan's dancing is symbolic; the symbolism is somewhat limited, artificial and literal. Her dancing, moreover, with some exceptions, tends to be static, an affair of postures and poses, and in some cases these postures are more learned than beautiful. Miss Denis is an imitative rather than a creative artist—that is to say, she attempts to interpret the East with both fidelity to the letter and the spirit, rather than to use its gestures freely, with the bold grasp of an artist, as elements of design. Her treatment of the East is in direct opposition to that of the creators of *Scheherazade* , who have been reckless of accuracy of detail, who have sought only for the materials to build up a gorgeous pattern, and have passed every concrete fact through the fire of a transforming artistic imagination. If, as has been said, the art of the future lies in a West that is conscious of the East, the recognition of the East will be in the manner of Monsieur Fokine rather than in that of Miss St Denis. Nevertheless, Miss Ruth

LEONORA

AS A SPANISH DANCER

Photograph: Dover Street Studios, Ltd.

St Denis duly ranks as one of the most cultured dancers of the time, and, in her special sphere, certainly the most learned. Her dancing is penetrated with the finest spirit of Indian art in much the same way in which Isadora Duncan's is imbued with the art of Greece. She has explored a new tract of the vast country which Miss Duncan opened up, and by interpreting the art of the East she has perceptibly broadened the scope of dancing in the West.

Probably those who are trying to revive the Classical Dance would succeed in getting closer to its spirit if they were to add to their study of the figures on ancient vases and frescoes an observation of the living Spanish dance of to-day. The gesture of a people has a more ancient and unchanging history than its speech, and it is unquestionable that much of the gesture of the ancient world has been preserved among the Spanish people, who still retain something of the inner spirit as well as of the outward circumstances of the ancient civilisation. Many of the poses found in the Greek figurines are essentially those of Spanish women; the play of the arms and hands, the sideward movement, the extreme backward extension of the head and body, are movements common both to the Greek and the Spanish dance. The castanet, which is invariably associated with Spanish dancing, was also used in Greece. The dancing that persists in Spain is almost certainly of a kind that was once common all round the shores of the Mediterranean. It has of course been modified by an Oriental influence, but it possessed its special characteristics long before the coming of the Moors. In the early days of the Roman Empire the dancers of Cadiz created a furore in Rome comparable to that which the Russians have aroused in the Paris and London of to-day.

Spanish dancing has been made familiar to French and English audiences by several dancers of repute, of whom the best known are Carmencita, Otero, Guerrero and Tortajada. There are some kinds of dancing, however, which are untranslatable into the terms of the art of other countries. The Spanish dance is intensely national. The snapping of the castanets, the short and insolent skirt, the exciting rhythm of the music, do not alone suffice for the performance of the *jota* or the *fandango* , as some foreign artists would appear to suppose; nor even when the dancer has caught the trick of the swaying of the hips, the lightning of the eyes, the arched back and provocative gestures, has she caught the spirit of the dance. She must first transform herself into a Spaniard. The Spanish dance depends almost wholly on personality; and not on the personality of the dancer alone, for it is one of those dances which seem to require an indefinable "rapport" between the dancer and the spectator. Mr Havelock Ellis has drawn attention to this feature in an interesting passage in "The Soul of Spain." One of the characteristics of Spanish dancing, he says, "lies in its accompaniments, and particularly in the fact that under proper conditions all the spectators are themselves performers. In flamenco dancing, among an audience of the people, every one takes a part by rhythmic clapping and stamping, and by the occasional prolonged 'olés' and other cries by which the dancer is encouraged or applauded. Thus the dance is not the spectacle for the amusement of a languid and passive public, as with us. It is rather the visible embodiment of an emotion in which every spectator himself takes an active and helpful part; it is, as it were, a vision evoked by the spectators themselves and upborne on the continuous waves of rhythmical sound which they generate. Thus it is that at the end of a dance an absolute silence often falls, with no sound of applause: the relation of performer and public has ceased to exist. So personal is this dancing that it may be said that an intimate association with the spectators is necessary for its full manifestation. The finest Spanish dancing is at once killed or degraded by the presence of an indifferent or unsympathetic public, and that is probably why it cannot be transplanted but remains local."

The success of La Carmencita was primarily due to this free play of personality which the Spanish dance permits. Mr John Sargent's picture, by which she will always be known to posterity, admirably displays the bold carriage, the somewhat defiant attitude, the suggestion of suppressed fire, which are characteristic of her type. As a dancer pure and simple, she was surpassed by many who never attained her wide reputation. She had gone through

LA OTERO

no inexorable training. She never pretended to any brilliancy of execution that was beyond her powers. Her manner was simple and unaffected. Without making any very strenuous efforts she glided through a few simple movements that showed off to perfection her supple and well-proportioned figure. She achieved fame less by the technique of her dancing than by her character, her allure, the distinction of her intriguing and exotic personality.

La Tortajada is a figure well known both in London and in America. Her style is not representative of the purest type of Spanish dancing, as it is apt to be infected with the atmosphere of the music-hall. Her personality, moreover, is far less interesting than that of La Carmencita. She was born in Granada, and her aim is to bring the warmth and colour of the sun of meridional Spain into her dancing—to dance, in fact, as she expressed it, "la danse ensoleillée."

"America," she says in a naïve account of her career, "has fêted me and showered dollars on me by the handful. Millionaires in particular have given me a great 'réclame,' among them Pierpont Morgan, Astor and Vanderbilt. The latter gave me a thousand dollars to dance one Christmas Day. Another American, Mr Taft, the future President, made a bet that I was taller than another woman well known to the public. He was at the pains of coming himself to measure me, and having won the five thousand dollars, he at once purchased a magnificent piece of jewellery with them which he offered to me. If the millionaires fêted me, so also did the poorest citizens of the Republic, the humble Sioux, who are still to be found in some of the wilder regions. While making a motor tour in the district of the immense pine forests for the benefit of my health, I fell in with some of these fine fellows and the idea suddenly occurred to me that I would dance specially for them. My husband and I improvised a stage and thereupon I danced my most voluptuous flamenca, which at first terrified but soon afterwards delighted them. I was royally rewarded, for the chief made me a present of some gold dust and a purse fashioned out of serpent's skin.... But the most curious spectators that I have known were three thousand Zulus whom I came across when motoring back from Johannesburg. Unlike the Sioux, they did not look on at my dance in silent admiration. No sooner had I begun to dance than the Zulus commenced to caper about all round me. Nothing could have been more picturesque, and at the same time more ludicrous, than the sight of a white woman in a mantilla appearing as mistress of the revels in a negro orgy!"

Guerrero is perhaps a more impassioned dancer than La Tortajada, but she has strayed even further from the purity of the Spanish dance. At the Marigny Theatre in Paris, she has this summer been dancing a new and startling dance called the Tango. It is a curious mixture of composure and frenzy, and at first acquaintance seems full of complications. Her rendering of it is said to take away the breath of the English and American tourists who fill the popular music-hall among the chestnuts of the Champs Elysée.

But the performances of these exponents of Spanish dancing only serve to show how swiftly it degenerates as soon as it leaves its native atmosphere. Even in the peninsula itself the dance seems to lose its essential character when it is performed in one of those palatial cosmopolitan music-halls, by the erection of which Spain is endeavouring to convince the world of its ability to keep abreast of the march of progress. To see the real classic dancing of an elder Spain, it is necessary to search among the shabby streets of the poorer quarters of Seville or Barcelona. There you may perchance discover some stifling, exuberant little café or theatre of the people, in which, if fortune favours you, you may find a dancer of talent, even of genius. I remember such an one in a little café chantant in Barcelona, no bigger and scarcely less unfurnished than a railway station waiting-room. The dancer appeared to be on the most intimate terms with the occupants of the stalls, and could at request lampoon the particular foibles of each habitué in *copletas* that were barbed with the cruellest Iberian irony. But her dancing had a brilliance, a fire, an abandon, and even a technical excellence, which I have never seen equalled in the displays of those artists whose names are known throughout Europe. It was at once

LA GUERRERO

Photograph: W. & D. Downey

expressive of the individuality of the dancer and of the race. It was as easy and as eloquent as Spanish speech. It was in fact the dancer's manner of conversing with the spectator, and it had all the daring, the wit, the provocativeness and at times the real poetry of her couplets.

It is little wonder that all the essential fire of the Spanish dance is quenched when it is performed upon the foreign stage. The atmosphere of Andalusia cannot be created in London or New York even by dancers of greater genius than Otero, Guerrero and Tortajada; and it should not be forgotten that Mr Royall Tyler, whose word upon the inner life of Spain must be taken as final, has remarked that "neither of those three ladies dances well enough to earn her living by the art in Spain. Their dances are intended for exportation into foreign countries where they are more appreciated."

CHAPTER XIV

THE REVIVAL OF THE MORRIS DANCE

N O view of the modern renaissance of dancing would be complete which did not take account of the revival of the Morris Dance.

Perhaps it has been too lightly assumed that England being a nation of shopkeepers has never been a nation of dancers. But shopkeeping is merely a habit, the product of circumstance, and in its nature a temporary makeshift. Dancing is a need of the spirit, a daughter of the high moods, and if, as Lucian said, it is as old as love, it is surely also as everlasting. The shopkeeping spirit may be, and probably is, antagonistic to dancing; but by the shopkeeping spirit I do not mean the modern spirit, for that is an incalculable, energetic and mobile thing, which is going to bear I know not what strange fruit in life and art. I mean that austere, unsmiling, level and practical temper which began to overshadow Western Europe some time in the sixteenth century; which set its face against ecstasy, and art which is the expression of ecstasy; which regarded poverty and vagabondage and unrestrained laughter as disreputable; which wor-shipped respectability, common-sense, such success as could be expressed in terms of cash, and all things that were materially substantial and endur-ing; which created Puritanism, the eighteenth century and the industrial revolution. To this temper, which found a secure lodgment in the Anglo-Saxon mind, dancing was naturally unsympathetic. But though it long held Britain, and America too, in its grip, it was not strong enough to strangle the free and joyous spirit which had created "Merrie England."

That spirit found its typical expression in the dance, and particularly in the Morris Dance. Not until the improbable event of the antiquarians arriving at unanimity will it be determined whether or no the Morris was originally danced by the Moors or "Moriscos" of Spain and imported by John of Gaunt into England in the fourteenth century; but if so, it was "diablement changé en route." It mixed with the native dances and was incorporated with a mass of Catholic and even pre-Christian tradition. In some English villages there are memories of a dance on the 21st of June, the longest day of the year, of a slaughtered ox, a procession in which one of the dancers carried a sword and a large wooden cup. To surmise what dim forgotten rites of a pagan sun-worship linger in this ritual would take us far into the labyrinth of archæology. But whatever its origin the Morris gathered unto itself the joy and holiday spirit of the countryside. It had its roots deep in the soil. It was inspired by the rhythm of an ancient, simple and full-blooded life, if not by the very rhythm of the woods and rivers themselves.

In spite of direct attempts at suppression, the inevitable desuetude of ancient custom, and the changed conditions of the life of the people, this dancing has come down from Catholic England to our own day. The Puritan preachers denounced it as "lewde" and "ungodlie"; but it survived even the tyranny of Cromwell's major-generals and flourished gaily under the Merry Monarch. In the eighteenth century it had already become de-moded. In a journal of the period we read of an account of a *soirée* , in which the writer said of a certain lady, with more candour than courtesy, that she "looked as silly and gaudy, I do vow, as one of the old Morris Dancers." In many villages, particularly in the west and south-west of England, there still exist "sides" of morris-dancers to whom the tunes and music have been handed down through an unbroken tradition. The fidelity of this tradition is in many cases surprising. Mr Cecil Sharp, to whom is chiefly due the rediscovery of the ancient dances, relates how he took down a tune from the fiddler of the Bidford morris-men which was identical, note for note, with one that he had found in a version printed in 1550. But during the last twenty or thirty years many of the old morris-sides have been disbanded. The revival has come at the eleventh hour. Already dances have been collected representing probably every variety of the morris-step; but in another generation the memory of the Morris Dance would have almost vanished from the countryside.

Soon after the Morris Dance took root in England it became incorporated with the old mummers' plays, which embodied the cult of Robin Hood. The traditional characters of Friar Tuck, Little John and Maid Marian accompanied the dancers. The hobby-horse and the fool, sometimes known as the dysard, provided the necessary comic relief. But the main interest, and a very serious interest it was, centred in the dancing. At one time almost every village possessed its troupe, and among the various villages there was a rivalry of dancing as keen as the rivalry of football to-day. Occasionally the contest became so hot that the victory was only determined by a vigorous bout of cudgelling with the staves, which served as an accessory in the dance. The Morris Dance was no hoydenish revel in which any unskilled yokel could take part. It developed an intricate technique which not unnaturally lent itself to the introduction of a kind of "star" system among the dancers.

Of these professional performers perhaps the most illustrious was a certain William Kemp, who achieved fame in Elizabeth's reign by dancing the Morris all the way from London to Norwich. He wrote an account of this feat in a pamphlet called "*Kemp's Nine Daies' Wonder* , performed in a daunce from London to Norwich: Containing the pleasures, paines and kind entertainment of William Kemp betweene London and that Citty, in his late *Morrice* ." In his droll and vivid manner he tells how at Sudbury "there came a lusty tall fellow, a butcher by his profession, that would in a Morice keepe me company to Bury. I gave him thankes, and forward wee did set; but ere ever wee had measur'd half a mile of our way, he gave me over in the plain field, protesting he would not hold out with me; for, indeed, my pace in dauncing is not ordinary. As he and I were parting, a lusty country lasse being among the people, cal'd him faint-hearted lout, saying, 'If I had begun to daunce, I would have held out one myle, though it had cost my life.' At which words many laughed. 'Nay,' saith she, 'if the dauncer will lend me a leash of his bells, I'le venter to tread one myle with him myself.' I lookt upon her, saw mirth in her eyes, heard boldness in her words, and beheld her ready to tucke up her russat petticoate; and I fitted her with bels, which she merrily taking garnisht her thicke short legs, and with a smooth brow bad the tabur begin. The drum strucke: forward marcht I with my merry Mayde Marian, who shook her stout sides, and footed it merrily to Melford, being a long myle. There parting with her (besides her skinfulle of drinke), and English crowne to buy more drinke; for, good wench, she was in a pittious heate; my kindness she requited by dropping a dozen good courtsies, and bidding God bless the dauncer. I bade her adieu; and, to give her her due, she had a good eare, daunst truly, and wee parted friends."

The Morris was sometimes danced, as William Kemp and his amateur roadside companion performed it, as a solo dance; but its most common characteristic was that it was danced by "sides" or sets of six. Women but rarely figured as performers. The dress of the men has become traditional, but it appears originally to have been merely the holiday dress of the period. It was marked by that "gaudiness" to which the captious critic of the eighteenth century took exception. The dancer was plentifully adorned with ribbons and rosettes, and latterly he wore the tall beaver hat which has become an essential part of the costume. The outfit was completed by the indispensable bells, which were stitched upon thongs and tied to the shins. Sometimes both treble and tenor bells were worn. In some of the dances the performers carried a white handkerchief and in others a short wooden staff.

In early times the dance was accompanied by a pipe and tabor, otherwise known as whittle and dub. The pipe was a kind of flageolet, which the minstrel played with the left hand; from his left thumb was suspended the tabor or miniature drum. These primitive instruments were superseded by the fiddle, which in its turn is giving place to the concertina.

The dance of the people is necessarily different from the dance of art. All national dances are characterised by vigour rather than

MORRIS DANCE: BEAN-SETTING

FROM *The Esperance Morris Book*

By permission of Messrs. J. Curwen & Sons, Ltd.

by grace. There is lurking in them a certain note of savagery and battles long ago. The old fighting England as well as Merrie England still lives in the Morris. It is not surprising that King Charles's men should have danced it on the eve of Naseby fight. It is essentially a dance for men, and a dance for the open air. It does not sway or glide; its movement is spirited and abrupt. The foot is lifted as in walking and then vigorously straightened to a kick; the heels come solidly to earth. The object of the dancer is to make the bells ring fortissimo, and to do this he must kick, and kick hard. The Morris does not exhibit the graceful postures and fawn-like agility of the Spanish country dances, nor the fiery energy of the Hungarian and the Russian. In its solid merriment, its even rhythm, its vigorous but restrained movements, it is essentially British.

It would be impossible to describe the spirit of the Morris Dance better than in the admirable words of Mr Cecil Sharp, who is not only learned in the history of the dance, but has sought it out wherever the tradition lingers on the greensward and under the ancient oaks of an England that is passing away. "It is, in spirit," he says, "the organised, traditional expression of virility, sound health and animal spirits. It smacks of cudgel-play, of quarter-staff, of wrestling, of honest fisticuffs. There is nothing sinuous in it, nothing dreamy; nothing whatever is left to the imagination. It is a formula based upon and arising out of the life of man, as it is lived by men who hold much speculation upon the mystery of our whence and whither to be unprofitable; by men of meagre fancy, but of great kindness to the weak; by men who fight their quarrels on the spot with naked hands, drink together when the fight is done, and forget it, or, if they remember, then the memory is a friendly one. It is the dance of folk who are slow to anger, but of great obstinacy—forthright of act and speech: to watch it in its thumping sturdiness is to hold such things as poniards and stilettos, the swordsman with the domino, the man who stabs in the back—as unimaginable things. The Morris Dance, in short, is a perfect expression in rhythm and movement of the English character."

The modern revival of morris-dancing in England is of very recent origin, but of astonishingly rapid growth. The story of its rise reads like a romance. This movement, which is already national in its scope, which promises to renew the heart of England, which is swelling out into wider circles that will probably be felt throughout the Empire and America, was born in a girls' club in a poor quarter of the north-west of London. The object of the Espérance Girls' Club in Cumberland Market was to bring something of the joyous and serene atmosphere of a younger and fresher world into the grim and hurried life of the city dwellers. For some time one of the features of the club had been the encouragement of music, dancing and play-acting. During some winters Scotch reels and strathspeys, Irish jigs and folk-songs, had been practised one night a week. A meeting between Mr H. C. MacIlwaine, the musical director of the club, and Mr Cecil Sharp, the leading authority on folk-music, led to the introduction of the English folk-song. From the folk-song to the folk-dance was only a step. Mr Sharp seven years before had collected a set of morris-tunes from some dancers in Oxfordshire, in whose family the Morris had been handed down from father to son for five generations. The idea suggested itself that as the girls had learnt to sing the old songs they might also learn to dance the old dances.

In October 1905 Miss Mary Neal, the secretary of the club, who has throughout been the directing spirit of the movement, went down to Oxfordshire and brought two of the morris-men up to London, and set them to teach the members of the club. The success of the experiment was immediate and astonishing. The girls were as unfamiliar with the steps and the music as with the speech and dances of ancient Greece; but perhaps a kind of ancestral memory awoke within them. The rhythms of the Morris had sprung from the rhythms of the old English life, and the Londoners, who are said to be never more than three generations from the soil, responded to a summons of the blood. Within half-an-hour of the coming of the Oxfordshire dancers the Morris, with its stamping of feet and clashing of staves, its maze of intricate movements, was in full swing upon a London floor. Thus was begun the revival of morris-dancing which to-day is a part of the national life.

The next step was the giving of a public concert to make known to the larger world the rediscovery of the ancient dances. This took place at the Small Queen's Hall in the following April. The public interest was immediately aroused. As one of the newspapers remarked with prophetic insight, it was "a little entertainment which may indeed light such a candle in England as will not immediately be put out."

From that time the movement progressed by leaps and bounds. Inquiries began to pour in as to how the traditional dancing could be brought back into the lives of the English people, to those in the towns who had lost it altogether as well as to those in the country for whom it was only a vague memory. Miss Neal's answer to this demand was to send out the best dancers among the members of her club to act as teachers. They have danced the Morris throughout the length and breadth of England. There is not a county to-day where the merry jangle of the bells and the clatter of the staves is not heard. In course of time the Board of Education took cognisance of the movement and introduced the Morris and other country dances into the curriculum of the elementary schools. In the spring of 1911 Miss Neal visited America, and by lectures and demonstration showed to the people of the new continent the old dances which their Puritan forefathers had omitted to bring with them. In response to numberless appeals for instruction she left behind one of the teachers of the Espérance Club, and the movement in the States is spreading with the same astonishing enthusiasm and rapidity as in England.

The most significant and hopeful feature of this movement is that it is in every sense a popular one. The inveterate cavillers may argue that it is artificially imposed upon the younger generation by a few cultured and enthusiastic pedants, and they will certainly repeat the well-worn shibboleth concerning the impossibility of putting back the clock. But the artificiality has been in the enforced imposition of a Puritan code that abolished dancing from the village green. To all healthy children it is as natural to dance as to laugh and sing. The tradition has been abruptly broken; now it is being restored to them and they respond to it with every fibre of their being. They are far from regarding it as yet another troublesome item in a bewildering system of education; they do not have to be driven to it as to a new species of drill. They revel in it as in a delightful game, for it satisfies all the child's inborn love of music and pantomime and emphatic rhythm. When once the initial impetus has been given from above, the movement goes on with its own momentum. Its motive force is not authority but the old indomitable impulse of the blood.

All that the revival of the old dances will do for the rising generation it is impossible to foretell. It is giving them back the power of self-expression, which the common people seem once to have possessed in the old days when music and song came naturally to birth in the life of the folk. As Miss Mary Neal has well said: "Music is the one art in which the otherwise inarticulate can express themselves, and so we have in this music the truest meeting ground for all classes. The revival and practice of our English folk-music is part of a great national revival, a going back from town to country, a reaction against all that is demoralising in city life. It is a reawakening of that part of our national consciousness which makes for wholeness, saneness, and healthy merriment."

The movement is at present still in its trial stage. If it becomes indeed a national revival of dancing it must result in a development of the dance. It cannot remain content with merely perpetuating an ancient formula. Every form of art which has the seeds of life in it must needs change and grow. The Morris, as has been said, was originally a men's dance, and already its performance by girls is changing something of its character. The introduction of the feminine element necessarily robs it of its sturdiness and at the same time lends it an added gaiety and grace. But the change will probably go deeper than this. The old Morris was the expression of a mode of life that has passed away; out of it must be developed some newer variation more fitted to express the spirit of a broader and fuller life. In a suggestive passage, Mr Holbrook Jackson indicates the direction of the development: "The old English folk-dances are limited in range; they are a combination of acrobatic leaps and hoydenish frisks. They are, indeed, the expression of a non-reflective and rather boorish peasantry. To-day conditions have changed. The peasantry are no more, and we have become introspective and reflective. The bumpkin and his kind have been replaced by the clerk, with a new set of needs and different nuances of desire; so that we have to consider not so much the question of reviving the dances of the past, because, as such, these can never be anything but curiosities, antiques, but how to pick up the lapsed tradition of the dance at the point in history when it expressed the emotions of the people, and to give that tradition a chance of new life in our own day; not a chance of imitating the past in form, but a chance of imitating the past in spirit, a chance of doing for to-day what it once did for yesterday."

The Morris cannot properly be called a dance of art; it is a dance of the people. It can never be a substitute for the dance of the theatre. But the popular revival of the old dances is important, not only in providing a new means of emotional expression, but in arousing a new interest in the art of the dance itself. Dancing is a sensitive plant which can only thrive in a congenial atmosphere. In some degree all the arts appear to live by the breath of popular favour. Their activity is stimulated, their expression perfected, by interest, criticism and understanding. The art of dancing has always risen to its highest level when it has been most esteemed; decadence has always succeeded to neglect. "Dancing is an art, let the public remember," a lover and critic of the dance has said, "which depends on their support for its very existence. The poet, the painter, the sculptor can work for posterity; but the dancer's art is fugitive, not permanent. If the contemporaries of any dancer fail through ignorance, or dulness, or bigotry, to appreciate her, no one else can."

If England becomes once more a nation of dancers, bigotry and dulness and ignorance will never again be obstacles to the flowering of the art of the Dance.

CHAPTER XV

THE FUTURE OF THE DANCE

"M EN are so unimaginative! My husband has all sorts of appliances for getting strong quick. He gets up in the morning and pulls at straps, twirls objects and kicks furiously at nothing. Such antics you never saw. Doubtless they have some underlying advantage or he wouldn't perform them, for he is a practical man. But they are so ridiculous. I always think of Don Quixote fighting the windmill when I see him threatening the air and striking absurd attitudes so seriously."

It is an American woman who speaks, and she speaks as the mouthpiece of a new idea—the attempt to recreate the lost rhythms of the human body by the means of dance movements. Not the least important of the results of the modern renaissance of dancing has been the rediscovery of the grace of bodily movement by the modern man and woman. The sight of the beauty of human motion on the stage has naturally suggested the idea of the introduction of this beauty into daily life. The dancing of Isadora Duncan, of Maud Allan, of Pavlova and Mordkin, has in fact awakened the ancestral voices of the blood; the spectator can no longer remain passive, but demands to be allowed to take his or her part in the cosmic measure. The speaker continues: "Now, when I get up and feel headachy or as if my body was stuffed with sawdust, I too have my exercise. But, oh, the difference! I start the 'Marche Militaire' on my patient phonograph, and the strains are so inspiring that I go through my paces so buoyantly that my husband stops his seesawing to enjoy my dance. Now the difference lies in this, that while I am unlimbering my muscles and starting my blood gaily through my veins, my heart and my mind are also uplifted with the rhythm of music and pose."

She then describes how when the patient phonograph is giving forth Mendelssohn's "Spring Song" she accompanies the music with a story related in motion and gesture. "I first point to an imaginary tree, run lightly to it, stretch up and pull down a bough, take it in my arms, then gaily throw it aside. This I do three times in different corners of the room. Suddenly I am attracted by the upspringing grass and trip lightly over it lest I crush it. Then I see flowers on the grass, sit down and gather an imaginary bouquet, then toss it over my head. This I do three times, and perhaps you may think it easy to sit down with one leg thrust forward and then break your pose gracefully in getting up. My mood changes. I hear a bird singing and bend forward to listen with one hand to my ear and my eye following its flight. Then I hear a bird in another direction and follow it. Three times these movements are repeated. The pose is now entirely different, the arms outspread as if in flight. I am by this time fairly enchanted with the spring and give myself up to the abandon of the moment, until my mood is exhausted and I calm down with music into final repose." At the conclusion of these exercises she remarks: "At this moment I feel as if every part of my body was enjoying an independent existence, but would, if I wished it, take a subordinate position for the common good. That is exercise as it should be."

The husband, we may suppose, is now thoroughly out of humour with his get-strong-quick methods. But where is his place in this new system by which the flexibility of the body and the exhilaration of the mind are sought in the movements of the dance? The dance, in any other sense than that of a ball-room accomplishment, is generally regarded as unsuited to the masculine character. How often has not one heard the remark that it is unpleasing to see a man dancer. And a man himself would as a rule rather be caught in the act of stealing than of dancing alone or with his fellows. The prejudice is new. It is perhaps characteristic of an artificial society for whose small conventions the liberal code of nature is too broad. In all simple and virile societies men have

MIKAIL MORDKIN

been dancers—unless some cramping moral code imposed its arbitrary prohibition—only in more decadent ages have they been content to be passive spectators. The men who fought at Agincourt, the men who fell in the Pass of Thermopylæ, were dancers. Greek manhood would not have been what it was without the dance. The Greek youths danced as simply and unconsciously as the Greek maidens, and they danced among themselves, singly and in groups. Nietsche said a wise word to this generation when he proclaimed his ideal: "Every man fit for warfare, every woman fit for children, both fit for dancing with head and legs."

America is seeking to discover a dance fit for men. It has found it in a translation of the movements proper to athletics, in an expression in dance form of all the masculine sports, a dance which women could not perform if they tried. A spectator who has seen an exhibition of this new method, which is clearly a revival of the old Greek method, has recorded that "the postures were those of wrestlers or swimmers, or runners or discus and javelin throwers, always preceded by the vigorous dance steps. And none of it was in the least feminine. It was dancing, but it was essentially masculine from start to finish. There was not a suggestion of airy grace; there was more than a suggestion of strength and rhythm and of iron muscles under excellent control.... Then," he continues, "I began to see the place of dancing in the world, its place as a wholesome natural recreation and as a form of physical training, more effective perhaps than any other, since a vigorous athletic dance brings into play nearly every muscle in the body. I saw that a normal enjoyment of dancing meant a healthy mind in a healthy body. There is no more sane and natural form of exercise than the rhythmic buoyant movements of the dance, performed with the vigour which men throw into it."

This form of dancing corresponds almost exactly with the Greek *gumnāzo* , which was the simpler and more exclusively physical of the two divisions of the dance, the groundwork for the *orchēsis* , the intellectual and emotional expression of bodily movement. The former provided the technique, which was to be mastered not for its own sake, but as a means of furnishing the body with that eloquence by which it could utter the moods of the spirit. Without this training in the dance, the Greek men and women could never have acquired that exquisite harmony, that easy grace of carriage, such as we see in ancient art. It may even be said to have made Greek art possible, for as J. A. Symonds remarked in his "Studies of the Greek Poets": "The whole race lived out its sculpture and painting, rehearsed, as it were, the great masterpieces of Phidias and Polygnotus in physical exercise before it learnt to express itself in marble and colour."

The modern revival of the dance will not do the same for the art of our own time until the dance becomes the common property of the people. For the ordinary man and woman dancing provides the simplest, the most natural, the most satisfying means of expression. Self-expression is a faculty the loss of which the modern age is just beginning to be aware of. An earlier age realised it in the arts of the folk—in folk-dance, in folk-song, in folk-lore and in the popular pageants of the Church. For its loss Puritanism is primarily responsible with its vulgar shamefacedness; it was further weakened by the Industrial Revolution, which broke up the old rhythms of social life; and it finally perished when our artistic pleasures became specialised and we chose to become passive, inexpressive spectators of professional artists rather than attempt any artistic expression of our own. Whereas a former age lived out its spirit in a popular music, a popular ballad literature and national dances, the present generation prefers to listen to the wheedling airs of the gramophone, to read a professional journalism and to watch a paid dancer in the music-halls. The tendency everywhere is for a passive enjoyment to usurp the place of an active participation in the arts. But the desire for self-expression is instinctive and irrepressible. In the dance it will find a means of satisfaction —complete, elemental, and one which has the saving quality of beauty.

By no means do I wish to imply that the dance of the theatre will ever be merged in that of the people, still less that it is desirable that it should. The dance of art demands the entire surrender of the artist's life. It is more than a pastime or a recrea tion. And as we demand that it shall become more and more expressive, so the study of the dancer must needs become more searching and minute. What new forms the dance is going to take, what new spirit is going to inspire it, only the future can show, but without pressing too far into the region of conjecture, it is possible to suggest the probable direction of its development.

In spite of the renewed vigour which the Russians have given to the ballet, it is difficult to believe that the strict, academic school of ballet-dancing has still a long term of life before it. Indeed the Russians—I am speaking exclusively of the Diaghilew company—have renewed the ballet by revolutionising it. Not only have they utterly transformed its spirit, but they have introduced a new manner and gesture. In *Cléopâtre* and *Scheherazade* how little remains of the strict technique of the classic ballet! The ballet is turning away from Milan and looking towards Greece and the East. Anna Pavlova has pointed out the way by which the academic style can find salvation. Her dancing is transitional. From the ballet technique it derives its precision and firmness of outline, but to these are added a fluency, a multitudinous play of the nuances of light and shade, a capacity for expressing an intense personal life. The fatal defect of the academic style is that it is impersonal. It is the geometry of the dance. If the personality of the dancer succeeds in disengaging itself, it is not so much expressed in the movements of the dance as violently imposed upon them. How drearily impersonal it can be, we are realising afresh now that the success of the Russian ballet has let loose a flood of indifferent ballet-dancers upon the stage. It permits a high degree of technical accomplishment divorced from the slightest emotional significance. It is the dance *par excellence* for the uneducated and unintelligent dancer—and it is she who must be banished from the stage. It justifies the gentle sarcasm of Pius IX. who, when asked for his consent to the presentation of a diadem to Fanny Elssler at Rome, assented, but remarked that in his priestly simplicity he had always believed that crowns were designed for the head and not for the legs. The famous Austrian dancer scarcely merited the reproach, for she above all other dancers danced with the head and the heart; but in general it is a just indictment of the ballet technique that it has disproportionately emphasised the importance of the legs and the feet. In the period of the decline of the ballet, the dancers of Paris and Milan in particular were little more than automata agitated by a pair of muscular legs, which worked with the precision and monotony of clockwork. The modern dance demands expression in every line of the body.

It is certain that the dance of the future will tend towards the fuller expression of personality. We shall not be content to watch dances that are merely dexterous, but only those that reveal a fresh and living emotion. It will follow that the dance must become infinitely more subtle, the body more responsive to the spirit, and the spirit more attentive to the delicate rhythms of life. It follows also that the day of the empty-headed, empty-hearted dancer, the simpering miss of the pink shoes and fixed smile, will be over. We will listen for what the artist has to say to us, and if she remains inarticulate, if she is unable to utter a syllable of poetry or of passion or of wit, we will politely ask her to trouble us no more.

In the future the content of the dance will be immeasurably enlarged. We shall learn that, like the ancient Greek dance, "it deals with every subject, grave and gay, religious and profane, decorous and indecorous; nothing in nature is too high or too low to be outside its scope; it embraces the whole scale of human passions." When it is grown to its full stature, the dance will probably combine with drama to create a new language for the imagination. *Sumurûn*, the production of Professor Max Reinhardt, is a type of a new art-form, neither ballet nor pantomime in the accepted sense of the words, of which the future is bound to see a further development. Its medium is gesture, but it is a gesture which, unlike the gesture of the old pantomime, is never merely a transcript of words. The twilight procession of figures to the palace of the Sheikh, moving with the rhythm of a frieze against the blank white wall, was no less than an event in the evolution of the dance-drama, pregnant with suggestive ideas. It presented movements and gestures utterly untranslatable into words, into painting or sculpture—untranslatable even, I think, into music. They were movements which had been caught up out of life itself, and fused by the imagination into pure symbols of beauty and delight, of pride and passion and wit.

The dance, I believe, is still only in its infancy. Is it rash to imagine that the evolution of dancing will be the special achievement of art in this century, as the evolution of music was in the last? There is a whole world of gesture waiting for the dance to take possession of. The rediscovery of the gesture of the ancient world is perhaps the least important part of the undertaking. There lies a broad field for exploration in the innumerable racial and national gestures, each with its separate beauty, and its separate expressiveness. And beyond this stretches the yet more inexhaustible do-

main of nature, its multitudinous minor rhythms, each various and distinguishable, merging into a grand rhythm of the whole, the eternal rhythm
of life itself. Fragments of attitude, phrases of motion, are scattered
prodigally up and down the world, awaiting the seeing eye and the understanding mind that can pluck these happy accidents, store them in the
memory, and at the proper time build up out of them a new pattern of
the dance. When the choregrapher of genius arrives, he will think in gestures, as the musician thinks in sound, and the painter in mass and colour.
And when he has realised the lavish abundance of his material, he will
pour into it like a molten flood all that there is in the brimming life of our
day to fire, to madden, to delight and to rive the heart.

Then it will be the turn of the other arts to look wonderingly upon
this figure of the Dance, no longer straying timidly into their company,
but coming upon divine feet, with an assured mien and a mature grace,
and each will borrow something from her ancient and untiring ecstasy.

INDEX

Table of Contents

Pylades, 46

Q

Quack M.D. , 82

Quadrille, 75

Quinalt, 29

R

Racine, 125 , 191

Radetzki, 49

Rameau, 29

Rayon d'Or, 94

Reichstadt, Duc de, 45

Reinhardt, Prof. Max, 220

Remy, Marcel, 111

Reynolds, Mr Rothay, 126 , 129

Richardson, Lady Constance Stuart, 119

Richelieu, 28

Rienzi , 60

Rimsky-Korsakov, 128 , 133 , 139 , 148

Rodin, 117

Roehrich, 141

Romanticism, 47 , 91

Rosai, 138

Rossi, Adelina, 62

Rubinstein, Ida, 146 , 158

Ruskin, 17

Russell, Countess, 77

FOOTNOTES:

[1] The use of the word "classical" to denote that class of dancing which claims kinship with Greek art is somewhat confusing. Before the recent revival, "classical" was the term applied to the traditional style of the ballet as distinguished from skirt-dancing, step-dancing and the various eccentric styles. To avoid confusion I have in general used the word "academic" instead of "classical" when speaking of the older school of the ballet.

[2] The late Sutherland Edwards proved himself a singularly accurate prophet when in 1881 he wrote: "We shall probably have to go as far as St Petersburg to discover a *première danseuse* worthy in some manner to be compared with those of twenty and twenty-five years ago."

Table des matières